DIPLOMATIC PASSPORT

For Moira and Doug.

DIPLOMATIC PASSPORT

More Undiplomatic Diaries, 1946–1962

Charles Ritchie

Charles Ritchie

Macmillan of Canada

A Division of Gage Publishing Limited

Toronto, Canada

Canadian Cataloguing in Publication Data

Ritchie, Charles, 1906-
    Diplomatic passport

Includes index.
ISBN 0-7715-9587-5

1. Ritchie, Charles, 1906-   2. Diplomats —
Canada — Biography.   I. Title.

FC616.R58A3   327.2'092'4   C81-094845-1
F1034.2.R58A3

Macmillan of Canada
A Division of Gage Publishing Limited

Printed in Canada

To
my friends in the Department of External Affairs,
past and present

Contents

Introduction

These journals, covering the years 1946 to 1962, take up where my wartime diaries, published as *The Siren Years*, ended. I ask myself the question, What is the compulsion that makes one put down on paper day after day such a personal record as this? Is it simply an exercise in egotism, or a confessional? Perhaps a little of both, but it may also be an obsession with the passing of time, a sense that life is slipping like sand through one's fingers and that before it vanishes completely one must shore up these remains.

It is said that every fat man has a thin man inside him, struggling to get out. Has every diarist a novelist inside him, struggling to get out? If so, the struggle is likely to be unavailing. The diarist, with his passion for the record — historical, social, or political — too often lacks the power of construction and the story-teller's skill. On the other hand, many writers are marvellous diarists but they tend to regard their diaries as the waste product of their art, material which is not yet fused by the imagination into finished work. Some diaries are written with an eye to publication as a conscious contribution to history. My own were of the private kind. It is true that in my old age I went public, or partly public, but when I wrote them they were for my eyes only. Nor are they at all like the informative memoirs of many of my contemporaries in diplomacy. Yet forty years in a career are bound to be conditioning, perhaps more than one realizes oneself, especially in a career spent for the most part away from one's own country, living the rootless existence of those to whom a place is not a home but a posting, shifting from one foreign capital to another. In this career the representational role tends to take over. The man sometimes merges into the ambassador. The result is not so much pomposity as a smoothness from which all angles and irregularities of temperament and opinion have been ironed out. From this fate diary-writing may have been an escape hatch for me. Diplomacy is a profession in which protracted patience, discretion, and a glaze of agreeability prevail, and it was a relief to break out, if only on paper.

This is the record of years spent in the foreign service of Canada, yet no official business was included in it. Here are to be found no breaches of the sacrosanct Official Secrets Act. From the Department of External Affairs in which I served I took no papers on departure. Buried in their archives is the evidence of my working life. This deliberate omission conveys a curiously lopsided picture, as though the writer, instead of being an industrious and reasonably competent official, had been a detached observer drifting idly about the world. An observer, yes — but what did he observe? Changing scenes and people, politicians, fellow diplomats and journalists, people of fashion or who sought to be so, authors and would-be authors, old aunts and young beauties, people labelled "interesting", and, often more interesting, those without a label. As to the scenes, they shift from Ottawa to Paris, from Delhi to Bonn, from London to New York, and always back to his native Nova Scotia. Thus the journal is an odd mixture of anecdote, reflection, politics, and personalities. It may be thought that this record is too personal for publication during my lifetime. The alternative of posthumous publication seemed to me a bleak prospect, so I let the record stand, with a word of advice to any fellow diplomatic diarist — keep diplomatic discretion out of your diaries and keep the diarist's indiscretion out of your diplomacy. A double life is doubly enjoyable.

1945-1947

In the years 1945 to 1947 the war was just over and the Cold War was just beginning. This was a time marked by one international conference and confrontation after another, at which East-West conflicts were accentuated towards the dreaded danger point of a third world war. Canada was represented at most of these gatherings, either as a participant or as an observer. While based in Ottawa I served as adviser to a series of Canadian delegations to such conferences, so that I was as much abroad as I was at home.

Despite the cloud of gloomy foreboding hanging over the future, these were, for a Canadian foreign service officer, exhilarating years. There was change in the air. Although the Prime Minister, Mackenzie King, was still governed by a caution verging on isolationism, another mood was beginning to prevail in the country. Our pre-war policy of no prior commitments had not saved us involvement in the struggle, and it was increasingly obvious that it was in our interest as Canadians to play our full part in the attempt to build a more sane and stable international order. I do not think that we in the Department of External Affairs approached the task with dewy-eyed illusions, but with a realization that whatever the frustrations, it had to be attempted. A further spur to a positive Canadian foreign policy was provided by the new pride and confidence in our nationhood, born of our achievements in the war and Canada's growing wealth and importance. No doubt, too, the temporary eclipse of so many great nations in Europe and Asia, laid low by the war, thrust Canada

3

closer to a front seat in the world community. These challenges and opportunities met with a ready and eager response in the Department of External Affairs, which was expanding in size and influence under the leadership of a gifted band of officials including Norman Robertson, Hume Wrong, and Mike Pearson. With the departure in 1948 of Mackenzie King from power, with Pearson as Foreign Minister and Louis St. Laurent as Prime Minister, both convinced internationalists, the political leadership came into being which could use the energy and talents to be found in the department to the full, so that our foreign service gained widespread international respect.

As a relatively junior officer I was only on the margin of decision-making. But there was a continuous interchange of ideas and opinions — rather rare, I think, in Foreign Offices — between the different ranks of our foreign service. We were encouraged to put our views on paper, not only concerning the routine work in hand but on broader questions, so that one had a lively sense of participating in policy formulation. Also, after so many years abroad, I was being inducted into the mysteries, the frustrations, and the techniques of life in a government department. "Power," as Mr. Churchill remarked, "is at the centre," and it was in those years that there was impressed upon me a lesson which I never afterwards forgot. No matter what your relations are with the foreign government to which you may be accredited, or whoever may be your political masters at home at any time, be sure that you are firmly entrenched in your own department and that your relations there are in good repair. Government departments have long memories; they sometimes forgive but they never forget.

Ottawa is a pleasant city. I had good friends and good times there. My work was interesting, yet I was restive. What more did I want? I suppose I shrank from the prospect of existence, year after year, as a completely adapted civil servant. I wanted to have one more fling at life outside the Victorian Gothic precincts of the Department. So that in January 1947 I welcomed the news of my appointment as Counsellor to the Canadian Embassy in Paris. There was to be a foretaste of Paris, as I had been named one of the advisers to the Canadian Delegation to the Peace Conference to take place there in August 1946.

The year that I had spent in Ottawa was one of those blissful intermissions from the servitude of the diary. Either I was too busy to keep it up or the diarist addiction had temporarily relaxed its grip, only to return in full force later, like other incurable addictions. Thus these diaries resume at the Paris Peace Conference.

The Conference was convened for the formulation of the peace treaties between the wartime Allies and Italy and the Balkan states. Its main focus was the controversy over the future of Trieste and the claims and counter-claims of Italy and Yugoslavia for possession of that city. Like all post-war international meetings, this quickly developed into yet another episode of the Cold War. The Canadian Delegation was presided over in a very unconvincing fashion by our declining Prime Minister, Mackenzie King. My own job, in addition to attendance at the plenary sessions of the Conference dealing with the Italian treaty, was to assist in the co-ordination of Canadian policies as prepared by our representatives on the separate committees dealing with the other ex-enemy countries. Our delegation stayed at the Hotel Crillon, in conditions of mingled splendour and inconvenience. It was the Prime Minister's favourite hotel and he had expressed a determination to sleep in the bed in which Woodrow Wilson had slept during the Peace Conference at the end of the First War. This involved delicate negotiations in inducing the hotel management to arrange the temporary expulsion of the lady who had for years resided in this suite. Even the apartments allotted to humbler members of the delegation, like myself, were those which before the war had been reserved for visiting sovereigns or peripatetic millionaires and, during the war, for German generals. (The salon of my own suite still smelled strongly of their cigars.) The hotel service was as urbane as it had been under the German occupation. The food was delicious; the telephone service, despite the presence of priceless antique telephones in every suite, was highly erratic. At times throughout the Conference we were isolated from other national delegations and totally cut off from telephone communication with Canada. Once, in a fit of exasperation, I determined to see for myself who the human agents were in the hotel who could be responsible for this confusion. I expected to encounter an array of overworked telephone operators; instead, I found one plump blonde lady placidly reading a magazine, with a box of chocolates at her side, facing a board on which light signals were frantically flashing from the different floors of the hotel. To these she seemed sublimely indifferent. "Where," I asked, "are your colleagues?" "I am alone," she replied, giving me a glance of pathos, as though she languished for company, even my own. The frustration of the Crillon telephone system seemed a fitting accompaniment to the frustration of the Conference itself. Met to consolidate peace in Europe, the former Allies were preparing the ground for further conflict.

Paris, August 21, 1946

The *Manchester Guardian* compares the Peace Conference to the situation described in Sartre's play *Huis-Clos*. Like the characters in Sartre's Hell, the nations are trapped by their own past actions and cannot escape. The situation is frozen. The delegates can only repeat endlessly the same arguments and the same gestures. Profound disillusionment and weary cynicism characterize all the delegations except the irresponsible and ebullient Australians.

Even the setting reminds one of Sartre's scene, which

was a salon furnished in gilt and plush, of which all the windows had been bricked up. We play out our Hell in the airless Second Empire salons of the Luxembourg Palace. How long is this interminable struggle of wills to go on? The Russians appear to be able to keep it up indefinitely. They have nerves, stomachs, and constitutions of iron. They give the impression of men who have no private lives. We western amateurs have not streamlined our lives enough; we are still in the horse-and-buggy age.

I shall think of this time as dominated by the game of trying to fathom Soviet intentions, of the tactics and strategy of power. International affairs have become a battlefield where the rules of war are relevant, and the strains on the combatants are as gruelling as on the battle-field. You need physical, mental, and nervous strength. But, hardest of all, you cannot afford too many distractions. That is not so bad for the old men who live only for ambition. It is hard on the young; they tire more easily and are more vulnerable to their own mistakes. The Old Boys have made so many that one more or less does not matter to them. Then the young ones have the other battles of love to contend with. They are fighting on two fronts. They must have time to sleep with their wives or someone else will do it for them.

August 23, 1946

In the evenings, when I come back after the day's Conference session is over, General Pope often joins me for a chat in the faded elegance of my hotel sitting-room, with its raspberry-coloured satin curtains. He is a delightful companion, witty and quirky. As Canadian representative on the Commission for the Peace Treaty with Romania, he is always stepping out of the line of his instructions. As we have few direct Canadian interests in the Romanian Treaty, he has been told that we should follow the British lead. He makes a point of doing the opposite. I

remonstrate with him, as I have responsibility for co-
ordination. "If you imagine that I am going to agree with
that soft-centred young prig from the Foreign Office, you
are much mistaken," he says. Then we differ about the
Nürnberg Trials. I say that such German generals as
ordered the massacres of civilians and other excesses
deserve to be shot. "And what about the German diplomats," he asks, "who signed documents resulting in
atrocities?" "It is different," I say, "for a diplomat to sign a
paper. Half the time he does not know what it may lead to.
That is not like giving an order to kill." "You and your
trade union," he says. "The fact is that the Nürnberg
Trials are scandalously unjust and should never have taken
place." He may be right.

The only fun I have at the Conference sessions arises
from the fact that I have been selected to maintain contact
with the Australians. Their Foreign Minister, Evatt,
whom we saw in action at the San Francisco Conference, *
has become insufferably megalomaniacal and irresponsible. He much enjoys undercutting any position taken by
the Canadian delegation. Like many Australians, he seems
to regard Canadians as mealy-mouthed fence-sitters. He is
also very jealous of any Canadian initiative or achievement.
Despite all this I much relish my contacts with the Australians. They are such pungently lively company and
don't give a damn for the proprieties. The New Zealanders
may be nicer but they are tamer.

The other day during the Conference session Evatt
made such an outrageous statement about Canadian policy
that on the spur of the moment I got up from my seat,
walked round the table to the Australian delegation, and,
bearding him in his lair, said that we must have an
immediate apology. He glared at me and I thought he was

*The San Francisco Conference opened in April 1945 and proceeded to
the creation of the United Nations. I was an adviser to the Canadian delegation.

going to knock me down. But he said nothing. A few moments later he came over to us and apologized profusely.

I have been reading *Darkness at Noon*, Koestler's novel about the Moscow Trials. The theme of the book is the tragedy of those who use unscrupulous means to attain great ends. It is a terrifying picture of the evil courses into which the Soviet bureaucracy has turned. Before the war one might have read it with the feeling that our humanitarian tradition was too deeply engraved for such dangers to threaten us. But can we be sure now? To defeat our enemies we used the atomic bomb, bombing the innocent, flame-throwing, commando tactics, and we imprisoned men without trial. Our newspapers toed the Party line on all these issues. When we were hard-pressed we were willing to use any means to attain our end — victory. Where was the humanitarianism of 1939 (war by leaflets — only the Nazis are guilty, not the German people, etc.) by 1945? So that our humanitarianism is of a fair-weather quality. It is born of stability and prosperity and dies with them. "Let us clear our minds," as Dr. Johnson said, "of Cant." But while we take a holiday from pity and morality in wartime and return to kindness and muddled thinking when the war is over, the Russians are in a perpetual state of war. How can we co-operate with such people? Only for limited and concrete purposes which promise joint advantages, and then watch your partner with a lynx-like eye. No other co-operation is possible. Does this mean that war is inevitable? At any rate it means years of unsleeping struggle for power. It means that all major decisions of foreign policy will have to be taken with an eye to this opponent. Fighting the Germans brutalized our methods of warfare to meet theirs; the struggle for power with the U.S.S.R. will brutalize our methods more and more. They do not believe in our morality for a moment. They think it clever hypocrisy. And after what we have suffered and inflicted in the last few years we are not so sure ourselves of our own moral superiority. Perhaps the Russians are just more logical than we, more brutally consistent. So often we can see, as in a distorting glass but still recognizable, our motives and actions reflected in theirs. We are more scrupulous, more gentlemanly, but how much does that difference matter? Sometimes, as over the scramble for bases, the difference seems to have narrowed down almost to the vanishing point. Yet that difference only divides us from the jungle world they inhabit. And the difference we must stick to — we must think it a strength, otherwise we shall be too much tempted to throw it over. We must demonstrate its effectiveness or we might as well disencumber ourselves of it and plunge nakedly into the struggle. Every act of hypocrisy in which our governments indulge weakens our own faith in that difference. If humane and fair political and social practices only spring from strength and not from fear, then we need to be strong — lest we give way to panic.

August 24, 1946
Fête of the Liberation of Paris.

The Prime Minister's forthcoming departure for Canada will be no loss to the Canadian Delegation and certainly not to the Conference or to the peace-making process. He has produced no ideas and no leadership. He just goes through the motions. He seems principally concerned with petty fiddle-faddle about his personal arrangements. However, if any member of the delegation leaves the hotel for a ten-minute stroll or to keep an official appointment, the Prime Minister senses his absence by some uncanny instinct and, on his return, subjects the absentee to a sad stream of reproach. "At one time it would have been thought a privilege to serve the Prime Minister of Canada. Now it seems that young people think only of their own pleasure." He insists for the record on keeping his personal expenses recorded at a derisory figure. I sat next to him in the Crillon dining-room the other night when he was consuming with avidity a lobster thermidor which must have cost twice as much as his whole daily expense account. He does not grow in stature in one's eyes. Brooke Claxton, the Minister of National Defence, will now take over as Head of the Delegation, which he has been in practice all the time. He has plenty of drive and ability, is most frank and friendly with me, and I like him very much.

The other day, during an interval in the Conference session, I was standing at one of the windows looking out at the sparkling fountains and patterned parterres of the Luxembourg gardens when I became conscious of a person standing beside me. It was Molotov, the Soviet Foreign Minister. He had removed his pince-nez and was wiping them clean with a handkerchief while gazing unseeingly at the scene outside the window. His eyes were red-rimmed, his face naked with fatigue. He looked like a weather-beaten Easter Island monument—but for a moment I had mistaken the old monster for a human being.

October 13, 1946
Bevin's* dinner at the British Embassy for Dominion delegations. After dinner Alexander, the First Lord of the Admiralty, played music-hall numbers of 1914 vintage and sea shanties. The party gathered around the piano and sang in a ship's-concert atmosphere of jollity. Mr. Bevin danced with Mrs. Beasley† of Australia, and they cavorted about like two good-humoured elephants. Here we all were—"the British family of nations". What a funny collection! The prevailing social tone of the evening was British lower middle class. Since Labour came in in Eng-

*Ernest Bevin, British Labour politician, was at this time Secretary of State for Foreign Affairs.
†Wife of the Australian Ambassador.

land they are the rulers — the politicians. Their servants of the upper class — the professional diplomats and officials — joined benevolently in the fun, taking the attitude "they are really rather dears and it is nice to see them enjoy themselves in their simple fashion and we must not seem patronizing," except for one who remarked to me, "This is where experience at Servants' Balls and Sergeants' Messes comes in so useful."

The Embassy staff of elegant young and not-so-young Etonians, and the sophisticatedly pretty young secretary of Lady Diana* (who had retired to bed with a toothache), had obviously fortified themselves for the evening with every drop of alcohol they could lay their hands on. I could picture the shudders in the Chancery at the idea of an evening with the Dominions, but it was Alexander and Bevin who made the party a success. They and the Australians are birds of a feather — all old trade-unionists together — members of the New School Tie — same standards, same jokes. You felt at once how English the Australians and New Zealanders are and how un-English the rest of us are: the South African, General Theron; the Indian, a fish completely out of water with his constrained, uneasy smile, being "coped" with by the wives; the Canadians — the Vaniers and myself — so different again.

October 15, 1946

Elizabeth Bowen† is here. She has got herself accredited to the Conference as a journalist. We meet every day in the fenced-off area of the gravelled terrace outside the Palais du Luxembourg, where the press are permitted to

---

*Lady Diana Cooper, wife of Duff Cooper, British politician and member of Churchill's wartime government, who was at this time British Ambassador to Paris. Lady Diana was herself a famous beauty and social figure.

†Novelist. She was a close friend from the war years (see my book *The Siren Years*).

mingle with the diplomats. We sit talking and drinking coffee at one of the small tables set up there and sometimes afterwards have time for a stroll along the tree-lined walks on the shady side of the gardens, past the statues of dead poets. She is staying around the corner at the Hôtel Condé, still unchanged as I remember it in the twenties, with its narrow stone stairways leading up to the garret bedrooms. We often dine together in one of the small restaurants on the Left Bank. Her being here is the reality which shows up for me the unreality of this sad charade of a conference.

Paris

The Diary for 1947 opens on my return to Paris as Counsellor of Embassy.

Our Ambassador to France was General Georges P. Vanier, later Governor General of Canada. He occupied a unique position in the diplomatic community in Paris. He had been a steadfast supporter of de Gaulle and of the French Resistance Movement from the outset. He enjoyed the trust and affectionate respect of French political leaders of varying parties and persuasions. They came to him as to no other foreign ambassador for advice. They confided in his judgement, integrity, and discretion. The Ambassadress, Pauline Vanier, a woman of distinguished beauty and warm charity of heart, carried all before her by her spontaneity. They were fervent Catholics, who lived their faith. French by ancestry, they loved France and believed in her future in the worst of times. As a new arrival at the Embassy I was treated by the Vaniers, whom I had known during the war, as a friend, almost as a member of the family. I much enjoyed working with the Ambassador; despite his distinguished military career he never seemed to me a typical soldier. He was sagacious and subtle, and I appreciated his particular brand of irony and deprecatory understatement, which often concealed a sharp point.

The work of the Embassy was interesting in itself but unrewarding in terms of results. We reported to Ottawa at length on the twists and turns of French politics and the recurrent ministerial crises of those uneasy years when France was still suffering the traumatic effects of defeat and humiliation. No one was better informed than the Ambassador about the French political scene, and he trusted me with drafting many of our dispatches home. Answer came there none. The Canadian government had at that time no discernible interest in France, or if they had, it was not revealed to us. I pictured the fruits of our labours mildewing in the files of some junior officer in the Department of External Affairs. Most of the staff of the Embassy were French Canadians. It was my first experience of working with them as a group, as in those days our department at home was almost entirely Anglo-Saxon in language and mentality. I was stimulated and attracted by my French-Canadian colleagues and made many friends among them, particularly the quick-witted and responsive Jean Chapdelaine and his delightful wife, Rita.

The Embassy was housed in a mansion in the Avenue Foch, erected in the 1920s for one, or both, of those fabled enchantresses of the period, the Dolly Sisters, by a wealthy admirer. During the German occupation it had been in the hands of the Gestapo—a centre to which victims were taken for interrogation. The décor, in pseudo-rococo style with inset bands of pink marble, must have been a sinister setting for the dreadful scenes enacted there. As an Embassy the house was superbly impractical. Typists were packed into passages and boudoirs. The vast marble bath with its solid gold taps was piled high with files and documents, which even overflowed onto the bidet. My own office was in the bedroom in which once the Dolly sisters had romped. My desk, an enormous affair in an unrestrained version of the Louis XV style, was rich in gilt and ormolu, with drawers that stuck when you tried to open them. It was placed between tall French windows looking out on the Avenue Foch.

My first task on arrival in Paris was to find myself somewhere to live which I could afford. Finally I installed myself in an apartment on the Boulevard St. Germain. The house was built round a paved courtyard. My own flat was up one flight of stairs. It belonged to the scion of a family who had owned a Paris department store. There he had lived with his mistress, a well-known actress. This happy state of affairs was brought to an end by the bankruptcy of the department store and by the intervention of his wife, who under some obscure provision of French law now claimed the flat belonged to her. He was determined that it should on no account fall into her hands, and to prevent this he must find a tenant, preferably a diplomat who could not easily be expelled. Our bargain was struck over a bottle of rye whisky, which he had never before tasted and to which he took an instant liking. Two conditions went with the lease: first, that his wife should never on any excuse penetrate into the apartment; second, that I should supply him each month with a case of rye whisky.

My apartment was on the dark side, which suited me, as I dislike brightness in rooms — or people. In fact there was so little light in the dressing-room that I often emerged wearing socks of different colours, sometimes even trousers that belonged to other suits than the coats. As one entered there was a stone-flagged hall with, on the left, a tiny dining-room suitable for dwarves only; on the right, a large and largely-unused salon in which spindly chairs and precarious little tables were grouped in uneasy circles. The parquet floor was islanded with dangerously slippery rugs. The salon led directly into the bedroom, the setting for a bed of generous proportions — evidently the scene of action of the whole apartment. Opening out of the bedroom was a small chamber containing a writing-table and an indispensable stove. The winters of 1947 and 1948 were cold ones and much of one's time was spent huddled for heat in front of the stove. I loved this apartment with the passion that some interiors have the power to induce. It had, it seemed to me, been a scene of happiness and I was happy there.

A further part of my bargain with the owner was the continued employment of a man-servant who "went with" the place. Yves was of an unguessable age — probably not so old as I then thought. He had started life on an estate in Brittany and had been brought to Paris as a gardener by the old countess who had once owned the whole house in the days when it had been an *hôtel particulier* and who still lingered on in the apartment below us. Yves himself lodged in company with a so-called nephew, a sloe-eyed adolescent, in an attic hovel above. He attached himself to me with bossy devotion, like an old nanny. With his full share of wooden Breton obstinacy he combined great tact — was never in the way at the wrong moment. He had at times a sly smile, conspiratorial without ever becoming indiscreet. He was an excellent plain cook in the provincial style — very good with soup and with a passion for the artichoke which I came to share. In the kitchen he mercilessly bullied a musty old crone who was never permitted to approach me directly but who could be glimpsed bent double over the sink.

My domestic life thus satisfactorily settled, and by no means overburdened with work, I set about determinedly to extract as much as Paris had on offer and to suppress my persistent traces of guilt at leaving behind me Ottawa civil-servanthood. I approached the Paris scene in the spirit of the Renaissance Pope who said, "God has given us the Papacy, now let us enjoy it."

Elizabeth Bowen came on frequent visits to Paris and her friendship which meant so much in my life continued, as indeed it did until her death in 1973.

Socially I moved in different circles which seldom overlapped, a condition which has always appealed to me. Through the friendship of the Vaniers I encountered most of the leading French political figures, also intellectuals like Jacques Maritain and André Malraux. Then there were my colleagues in the Embassy and my fellow diplomats. I had friends among the journalists—the closest, Darcy Gillie of the *Manchester Guardian*. Another world was that of the English and American friends who flocked to Paris after the long deprivation of the war, eager for a renewal of the pre-war pleasures of which they had been so long deprived. There was a continuing cavalcade of such visitors with whom the more cosmopolitan French mingled. Some of the actors and actresses in this revived social perform-ance were getting older, but there were spirited recruits from a younger generation. The Parisian arts and fashions —it was sometimes difficult to draw a line between the two (a "New Look" by Dior, a new stage design by Bébé Bérard)—enlivened the scene. Party succeeded party— fancy-dress parties, picnic parties, dinner parties, theatre parties, and house parties. Pre-war social rivalries revived, wits were sharpened, scandal took wings, and love affairs came and went as brief as summer lightning. At the British Embassy, Duff and Diana Cooper reigned—there politicians, writers, and artists mingled with the fashion-ables. Under Diana's magic touch, platitude and pompos-ity shrivelled—all was warmth and sparkle.

January 20, 1947

Well, here I am back in Paris and installed as Coun-sellor of Embassy, but why the hell am I here? What possessed me to leave an interesting job, in which I could exercise some influence on events, to walk up and down the Champs-Elysées on a sunny day or to admire the beauties of Paris. Life is not a coloured picture-postcard. As for my work at the Embassy, what do they care in Ottawa for a painstaking analysis of the shifting play of French politics and politicians? Anyway, French politics, although absorbing on the spot, do not export well and are incomprehensible outside France. D. W. Brogan once spoke of "the provinciality of the *Ile de France*". It is quite true. Then, returning to the Paris of my student days as a middle-aged official is like paying a social call on a former mistress. I think of the desolating scene in which Colette's Chéri revisits Léa, when the nostalgic disturbance of his love for her and the shock of his war experience are met with her sensible health recommendations. Yes, Paris has only a bitter little smile for the past. Sufferings and scarcities have contracted her spirit. She has become a *femme de ménage*.

February 1, 1947

Elizabeth Bowen is here. The weather is so penetratingly cold that we spend most of the time sitting close by the stove in my flat, often in company with a bottle of whisky. It is like life on board ship. We sally out on to the windswept decks of the boulevards for a blow and are glad to be back again in the warmth and shelter. I want to see no one else and wish that this good time could last, yet feel that it is transitory. She re-awakens my sympathy for people, my curiosity about situations and ideas; she re-humanizes me.

February 7, 1947

The smell of dusty ivy on a misty winter's afternoon as I go past the enclosed gardens of the big, shuttered houses in the Avenue Foch.

There is nothing in the least mysterious about the French. It is just that they are plainly different from us and for that very reason attractive and somehow formidable. They are gay, but not funny; they make one smile but not laugh; they are so conventional in the grooves of custom, however revolutionary their ideas may be. They have no use for eccentricity — you must be effective in the life here or you are mercilessly brushed to one side. They never tell a story against themselves. After all, why reduce your bargaining power by giving the world a handle against you?

March 4, 1947

During the war we had a simple poster-picture of what was going on on the European continent. It seemed to us an armed camp of enemies — German bullies and satellite zanies — lording it over a vast concentration camp of subject peoples and defied by numerous and heroic resistants. We had to believe that things were black and white; in a war it is a dangerous waste of energy and sapping to the will to admit that one's enemies have mixed motives and sympathies, but it is interesting to take off the wartime blinkers and to indulge in what still seems an unpatriotic luxury of seeing people not just as friends or foes but as people. It leads one to all sorts of reluctant and awkward admissions.

Today, for instance, I spent at Versailles at Beaudoin's trial. He was the Vichy Foreign Minister. It is gospel that the men of Vichy were odious, but there simply did not appear to be any evidence against him at all. I said to myself that I disliked the man, that he had played both sides, that he was anti-Semitic, anti-British, anti-Resistance, a careerist and probably a crook, one of those who had stifled the soul of France. But I could not say, on the evidence produced in court, that he was guilty of any of the precise things with which he was charged.

Evidence came from so many sides, from honest men who had worked with him and whose own reputations were clear, from British Intelligence, from a Free French Jewish fighter pilot. All coincide with remarkable accuracy — he was a patriotic Frenchman who had done his duty as he saw it and, given his own aims, quite effectively. Obviously if he is condemned on that evidence it will be a miscarriage of justice.

March 27, 1947

Mathieu, the Corsican chauffeur at the Embassy, has become almost a friend. He is a man of thirty-five to forty, fat from good eating, and he likes to hear the sound of his own voice, loves a joke, and has immense confidence in his own opinion on all subjects. He can put on a tough, taxi-driver manner and a coarse, rough voice whenever the need arises in the traffic. He takes me out to Versailles to the Beaudoin trial. He misses no points in the trial — in fact, he catches several that I missed. But what first endeared him to me was our common passion for *The Three Musketeers*. He said he had read it at an age when he still believed in love and friendship. I like the way he said that, without bitterness, with a grown-up acceptance of life. Of "Milady" he said, "She is just the woman to excite a boy's imagination — a woman of the world, seductive and so beautiful." (Milady's beauty is indeed one of the unquestionable facts of literature.)

The feeling of liberation that I get in France is because anything can be discussed here and quite naturally too. I can talk about women with Mathieu (the chauffeur) or I can talk about doctrinal differences between the Church of Rome and Protestantism. When he talks about women he does not give me commercial travellers' stories; he talks like an individual, and if he talks about religion it is not to air a few prejudices but to *discuss*. Marcel, the other chauffeur, tells me of how he was put in a German concentration camp and how the older men in the camp went to pieces and wept with despair. "Indeed, I admit that I wept — it was not that I was frightened, but to find myself in prison with armed sentinels, knowing oneself to be an honest man, was enough to make one despair. All the old men were like that but the young ones joked and did not give a damn." What Englishman would tell anyone that he cried when he found himself in a prison camp? He would think no one else had ever done such a thing. The French are not ashamed because they have not set themselves an inhuman standard of behaviour. They are natural men — not public-school boys, or American tough guys, or Nazis, or communist supermen, but natural men.

April 3, 1947

Anne-Marie Callimachi* is here on a visit from London. She talks of Romania, from which she was clever enough to escape in time, saying that a communist takeover is richly deserved by her own class, that they have been corrupt and rapacious. However, she still manages to get substantial slices of her fortune out of that country. She is bored with my interest in French politics and says that Paris is the worst place to find out what is happening in Europe, as the French are so self-engrossed. She claims to be in a state of suicidal depression but appears in high spirits, buying new hats and a Modigliani painting, and up to her ears in mysterious financial deals through her banker in Switzerland. We talked of the erotic effects of train travel, due, we think, partly to the motion of the train itself, and always seeming most insistent on the night train from Paris to the Côte d'Azur.

May 5, 1947

The green arches of the park of Chantilly in the April sunshine, the blowing of the paper tablecloths into the grounds of the Lion d'Or, the taste of pâté and red wine warm from the sun, and the sight of M. standing beside the car, her plaid rug over her arm. She scowled into the sun. She is like a statue carved in ivory, her beauty severe and classical. What a fool I am at forty—adolescent dreams that have been dreamed too long.

May 6, 1947

Lunched with Darcy Gillie of the *Manchester Guardian*. He lives with and for books, as a cat-lover might live surrounded by cats. You stumble over insecurely piled pyramids of books when you go to his room. He has a noble

*Princess Anne-Marie Callimachi was a refugee from Communist Romania. Formerly she had been a wealthy political and social hostess in Bucharest.

cast of countenance and a nature devoid of smallness. I admire and envy him. I wish I knew as much about anything as he knows about North Africa — and never to be boring about it. Yet today he was suffering from a hangover and was less intelligently articulate. I find people more attractive when they are not in "good form", and I felt positive affection for him when, scrabbling among his papers, he cast over his shoulder at me "What year is this? I find it hard to keep up with the revolving years." M. was here in the evening. It was not a success. We had dinner on a small card-table with uneven legs which Yves attempted unsuccessfully to level. I could see that she disconcerted him by bleak glances at the arrangements of the flat. She is beautiful and intelligent, but have we anything in common? I asked her if she felt with me as if she were talking to someone of another generation and had to get me going on a favourite subject, spot my hobby-horse, and send me off on it. I used myself to do that with older people while cooking up in my mind the unscrupulous schemes of youth. Is she doing the same?

May 7, 1947

Elizabeth de Miribel is an extraordinary personality. I have known her since the war years in Ottawa, when she, an exile from France, with a handful of others upheld the Gaullist cause in Canada with missionary zeal and in the face of all odds. Back in Paris, she now occupies an influential position in the Quai d'Orsay. In everything Elizabeth is larger than life-size — in her range of interests and friends and, above all, in her fanatical enthusiasms. She is out of scale with compromise. The most loyal of friends, she is a despiser of the middle road. She has just come back from Moscow full of the spiritual qualities of the Russian people. "They are so much richer spiritually than the Americans. Their faces are more interesting. There is still a continuity with an old and great civilization which has not been entirely lost to communism." I even fancied that a new way of doing her hair showed Russian influence — it suited the earnest, poetic young woman in a Russian novel and was less Princesse de la Fronde than her usual coiffure.

May 8, 1947

The Poles invite us to the magnificent Hôtel de la Rochefoucauld which is now their Embassy. Course after course of rather badly prepared food. The Ambassador — squat, voluble, formerly a schoolmaster in Cracow. Reception afterwards — hordes of swarthy Eastern Europeans — thug intelligentsia who look as if they could shoot as fast as they can argue — swarming like termites through the lofty rooms. These cocktail parties and official receptions where dull and tired officials are crowded with tiresome women into brilliant rooms made for leisure, for conversation, for the mannered comedy of intrigue! Clumsy attempts of the state robots to be gay!

May 9, 1947

I had John Grierson, formerly of the Canadian National Film Board, to lunch. He talked about his interest in economic freedom and his belief in a cultural aristocracy — how he was always being asked to lecture on aesthetics when he was really a political scientist. He twisted up his eyes hypnotically behind his spectacles to give me glances of piercing insight. He spoke of the Prime Minister as an "old darling". Grierson is working in UNESCO. What a stew-pot of jealousies UNESCO sounds. God preserve me from having anything to do with it. One look at the people at the UNESCO building was enough. How I loathe international secretariats — they are always so provincial — talking shop all the time and having affairs with unattractive secretaries. They think they are "men of good will" and progressive. They make no allowance to themselves for their egotism and love of power. They have no humility. I am sure the League atmosphere at Geneva would have made a fascist of me.

In the evening at Paul Beaulieu's,* a reception for French-Canadian intelligentsia—a world new to me of young French-Canadian students, artists, and actors who are finding Paris for the first time and who have a whole set of new gods unknown to me. Young students came up to me greeting me with great charm as *Monsieur le Conseiller*, and getting away as quickly as they prudently could to continue passionate discussions among themselves. But they *do* have passionate discussions and they are infatuated with ideas and phrases. And everyone was enjoying just being there and *talking*. After the aridity of diplomatic entertainments and the suspicion which ideas, especially ideas about art or literature, arouse in a group of Anglo-Canadians, it seemed all to be a Good Thing.

Reading Shakespeare's *Romeo and Juliet* — one could get caught in Shakespeare and spend one's whole life (and it would not be long enough) in that world of clues and whispers, glorious vistas, sweet songs and perfumes, breath-taking glooms — in that world so monstrously larger than life.

Date Most Uncertain

Weekend in the country with the d'Harcourts — nice French people — in fact, impoverished gentry. A small, shabby château of no particular period (1820-1830?) with bowls of lilac everywhere — in the halls, in my bedroom — so that the whole house smelled of it. They had Germans in the house during the war but it must have been shabby long before that. No signs of a bath anywhere, primitive

---

*Paul Beaulieu, an officer of the Department of External Affairs and subsequently Canadian Ambassador to France.

W.C., but of course a brand-new glistening bidet. They are a very nice family and I liked them all. Comte d'Harcourt takes rather a back seat. His wife is much concerned with local affairs — she sat on some local women's council with a communist woman councillor. She said, "At first the woman was impossible, she must have this and must have that — but she is getting better — already one has got her to use the conditional mood when discussing business and I am lending her some good religious books." This pleasant-looking couple have produced two buxom daughters — short, stocky, peasant types — very nice, simple, and natural (which did not prevent one of them from showing off like mad). Then my friend Emmanuel, their nephew, was there with a sister, a shade less buxom but giving off a slight odour of "good works in healthy country surroundings". On Sunday morning they all went off to Mass and I made a tour of the park, which is encompassed by a high wall. It was a shut-in world of rough grass, trees, and rides in the woods, quite thick undergrowth with violets and other small violet-coloured flowers everywhere. I lay on a cut log in the sun and felt extremely happy.

May 15, 1947

Dined with Maurice Forget (our Military Attaché) to meet General Revers, a famous figure of the French Resistance — his idol. He gives the impression of being deformed due to his immensely broad shoulders and his jutting, underhung jaw. He has charm and quick wit — he is bold, magnetic, vain, and intelligent — in conversation, half-jokingly cynical and extremely outspoken. The company consisted of his wife, another general (retired), who had at one time been in charge of the French Deuxième Bureau and who, in appearance at least, was (to me) a most baffling type, a "simple soldier", and General Revers's Chef de Cabinet, who has been with him in all the changes

of fortune in the Resistance, etc. — a sloppy, clever, intellectual soldier. Most of the conversation turned towards
North Africa, as Juin had that day been appointed Resident General in Morocco. General Revers said that the way
to preserve the balance there was to set the Berber against
the Arab. For thousands of years the Berbers had been in
the habit of making raids from time to time on the rich
Arab towns. Now was the moment to let them have a go
at, say, Fez — the Resident General could shut himself up
in the Residence, a little massacring would go on, and
after that the French would have no difficulty with the
Arabs for some time. As for the Sultan, it was only
necessary to back another candidate for the throne to put
the fear of God into him. These ideas were advanced with
cynical cheerfulness. Maurice Forget says they are quite
serious and a Berber rising is just what the French will
arrange.

After dinner a young French deputy from North
Africa and a French North African newspaper proprietor
joined us. The conversation which followed on North
African problems was something of an eye-opener to me.
Here was a group of men completely sure of themselves,
with none of the shaken confidence of the metropolitan
Frenchman. To them the Arabs are simply an inferior race.
They say that there is no good providing them with
improvements — they prefer living in pigsties, and when
decent houses were built for them they turned them into
pigsties. There is no use paying them more — they have no
sense of the value of money; they spend it at once and sit in
the sun doing nothing until they are hungry and then work
again for a little. The inhabitants of the towns were
Semitic in origin and therefore, of course, cowards. All
that was needed in North Africa was, as Lyautey* used to
say, to show strength and then you would not have to

*Maréchal Lyautey, French soldier and administrator in North Africa.

employ it. All would be well if (a) the French socialists would leave the situation alone, and (b) the British and Americans would mind their own business and not meddle. For the British there seemed precious little sympathy. The British had intrigued to drive them out of Syria — for that (as the French always say) there is documentary proof. The British had invented the Arab League for their own nefarious purposes and it was a source of some satisfaction that they were now having trouble with it. As for the Americans, they were always prating about democracy but look at the way they treated their Negro population.

August 10, 1947
    Paris in mid-August. Weak, plaintive music coming out of a courtyard as one passes by — the houses with all their shutters closed — no one left but concierges and their cats — the Luxembourg gardens under a hot mist blazing with sunset colours of orange and yellow dahlias — a thin jet of fountain. No one to see all this summer luxuriance of foliage and flowers but a few children left behind for some particular reason in Paris — and an old woman in carpet slippers and a scowling gendarme.

August 11, 1947
    Picnic organized by Diana to an eighteenth-century folly — La Tour de Retz — now tumbling down and overgrown with ivy, the garden a wilderness of brambles and wild roses. Diana and Cecil Beaton (echoes of how many *fêtes champêtres* of the twenties) suited the place as they draped themselves about a crumbling urn. Duff, who hates picnics, kept wishing that he had a little folding chair to sit on. "How can you!" cried Diana. "To take a chair to a picnic."
    Had dinner at the British Embassy. More moments of nostalgia — the Gay Old Times embodied in that

antique marionette Lady de Mendel,* who still slaps her thigh, kicks up her heels, and smiles with her eyes at eighty-four. "And from that dainty little jewel such a whiff of garlic," said Cecil Beaton. I asked Diana if she remembered my Uncle Harry.† "My first love—he lived opposite us in Arlington Street. He paid me my first compliment when I was a little girl—he wrote me a farewell letter before he died. I heard of his *dash* from my father." "What did he look like?" I asked. "My dear, *then* a death's-head."

Nancy Mitford to dinner—talking of the horrors of her country childhood—the boredom, the waiting around for something to happen. She said her grandmother used to change the hours of meals in despairing attempts to make—now the afternoons—now the evenings—shorter. "All those women in tweeds taking their cairns for a walk —waiting to die."

As I was driving to the office the other day I saw Nancy walking by herself past the bookstalls on the Quai. She had a floppy old hat on and looked not at all like her smart self, but pale and abstracted, and as she walked her lips were moving. She was talking to herself. She must have been trying out the shape of some scrap of dialogue in her novel. One could hardly believe she was the same person who appeared at dinner last week, her face then brilliant with animation, with that mocking turn-down of the mouth and the eyebrows lifted in incredulous amusement. Then she got into one of her spirals of talk, starting from a mere particle of absurdity that she had spotted in someone and cascading into a fantastic fireworks of invention, in which malice was so mixed with sheer high spirits

*Elsie, Lady de Mendel, fashionable interior decorator and hostess. Her husband, Sir Charles, was an honorary attaché to the British Embassy.

†H. K. Stewart, C.M.G., my mother's brother. He was a Gordon Highlander and King's Messenger.

and comedy that one couldn't call it malice any longer. What a sparkler she can be. How gloriously funny, but I should not relish being the mark of one of her arrows. Then there is, too, in her an undercurrent of bitter, scornful sadness, much less evident now than it used to be in London. Now she is on a crest with literary success, happy love, her charming apartment, and the most stylish clothes in Paris.

September 14, 1947

Lunch with André Malraux, Elizabeth de Miribel, an American journalist, a Swedish journalist, and Catroux. The American journalist crystallized the conversation by asking A.B.C. questions about Gaullism and French politics. Malraux, snorting and snuffling and sweating, replied with a flood of exposition. I am still left, at the end, with the feeling that after the party was over and the juggler had completed his act, when I came to count the teaspoons several of them were missing altogether. Or, to put it a different way, as the Swedish journalist said to me afterwards, "What worries me is that I think that sooner or later these people will get into power and then what kind of a job will they make of it?"

The American was interested (as a "liberal" journalist) to hear a convincing denial of the accusation that de Gaulle is a future dictator. He supposed that Malraux was a liberal too. Reply—"I fought enough to show it." Elizabeth (explanatory): "Monsieur Malraux fought in the Spanish Civil War." The American (incredibly but in good faith): "On which side?" Malraux's answer to the question as to whether he feared power being concentrated in the hands of one man was to say that nothing had ever been achieved in France except through the predominance of one man, and cited Clemenceau, Briand, and Poincaré. (This seemed odd to me as they had functioned under the old Third Republic Constitution and in a régime where there were more parties in France than there are today.)

Malraux thought that there would be no civil war in France unless orders for one came from Moscow; then, with great rapidity and staggering indiscretion, he gave us a map of France in civil war (the Gaullist civil-war map — what a break for the Communist Party and before two foreign journalists and one diplomat!). Here it is: the North, the Northeast, the frontier as far as the Somme — Gaullist; the coast down to and including Bordeaux — Gaullist; Boucles du Rhône — "plutôt Gaulliste"; Paris — Gaullist; Paris suburbs — Communist; Limoges — Communist; the South — Communist; Franche-Comte and Les Landes — a mystery. (In all this he seems to assume that the Socialist Party has ceased to exist and doubtless the M.R.P. too.) It was, he said, a geographical problem, just as the Civil War in Spain had been, and he quoted examples of whole Spanish provinces and regions on one side or the other. He remarked that there was an interesting parallel with the wars of religion in France — the areas of France which had been Protestant then were the areas which were Communist now.

He said that de Gaulle would come to power as a result of financial chaos and collapse. On being asked whether in those circumstances it would be better for the United States to wait to give aid to France until de Gaulle was in power, he first said, "In any case you will give too little," but finally said, "By giving aid in doles now you will only prolong the agony. Ramadier cannot cope with the situation. The United States should choose one party or another. You must disabuse your compatriots' mind of the idea of Right — Left — Centre, with de Gaulle at the Right. That corresponds to nothing real." In fact he was actively discouraging United States aid to France — doing just what we are always accusing the Communist Party of doing — preferring the interests of his party to those of

France because he believes that only under his party can France be saved.

Asked about de Gaulle's programme when he comes to power he replied: "We have two plans, one for the *relèvement* of Europe and the other for the *relèvement* of France. France can support herself—the only country in Europe that can." Malraux went on: "France can live off her own resources and is self-contained in a way that Britain is not, is a better bet than Britain for United States support." The barefacedness of this annoyed me.

Malraux impressed me as superficial—a man of letters dabbling in politics. I have no faith in his judgements.

September 15, 1947

Lunch and afternoon at Elsie Mendel's house at Versailles. Décor so familiar to readers of super-glossy fashionable magazines—very pretty it is too. Our hostess was spry—the skin on her antique face stretched like a too-tight ivory-coloured kid glove and the look of death in her eyes, but smart as an old monkey. I got through layers—eighty years—layers upon layers—a millennium of extinct civilizations, through the Roman and Etruscan periods to the Neanderthal woman—when she said that she (or was it her father?) was born in the old de Wolf house in Wolfville, Nova Scotia. It was a really Mendelian party: the little Queen of Yugoslavia; an American half-Cherokee Indian—"You know" (challengingly) "I never say anything behind people's backs that I would not say to their faces. I make a hobby of houses; I have one in Mexico, one in Virginia, one in California, a penthouse in New York, but best of all I like my house in Paris and my little château in the country." When jewels were mentioned—"I have a ceinture of emeralds—so amusing." I sat next to Greta Garbo, but all she said to me was "Pass the salt." But she said it in those husky, mysterious, palpitating tones that have echoed around the globe! She was wearing a

Mexican-style straw hat and everyone kept on begging her to take it off. She refused until she went into the swimming-pool and then one saw how clever she had been. It concealed both her beauty and the ravages in it. She still has that mixture of gaucherie and mystery and that lovely, lovely face. There were half a dozen Hollywood directors or producers, all more or less stout. Also Paulette Goddard, dripping with diamonds—just a gay, pleasant little American housewife, but in the same swimming-pool with Garbo she just did not rate. Old Sir Charles Mendel would not agree. "Wonderful bone structure Garbo has," he said, "but I like flesh—give me Paulette." "Yes," he went on, "I have what Elsa Maxwell would call 'my most intimate friends' here today—intimate acquaintances, that is what *I* would call them. I am a man with a lot of intimate acquaintances." All the people there seemed names out of an old *Vogue* magazine and all *so old*, except the immortal Tony Porson bounding about in the pool like a Neapolitan diving boy.

September 18, 1947

What answers have we to the questioning classes: the poor—the discontented—the young—the clever? One cannot think of the question in terms of "we North Americans" and "they Europeans". It applies to the democratic, anti-communist parties within the European countries. In France are those parties just a front behind which the bourgeois and the racketeers can, in their different ways—respectable or non-respectable—get on with their business? Are they so keen on their short-run interests that they have not even the intelligence and self-restraint to unite to secure their long-run interests? What about the alternative of Gaullism? What are its ideas? Improvement in the machinery of the State to make it stronger, but what is the object of the Gaullist State to be? A revival of patriotism—but is it to be patriotism in the raw or patriotism guided towards the evolution of the State in some advancing direction? A bulwark against communism? But what is on our side of the bulwark? If all our Western democratic civilization can do in Europe is to enable people who are already comfortable to go on being comfortable, *it* won't do. This civilization was sick in Europe long before the war — ever since the First War. Are we seriously bent on curing it or is it a question of enlisting "any allies of whatever origin" against communism?

December 7, 1947

Went yesterday to Nellita's wedding* in the Protestant Temple at Poissy — the cold, plain, bare little shrine of a once-persecuted sect. A star pastor had been brought down from Paris for the occasion — a true offspring of Calvin, his mouth a bitter line, eyes of dark fanaticism, twitching hands raised in blessing — a man of spiritual arrogance and probity. The service was very different from the cozy old Church of England or the solid smugness of Presbyterianism. Here the fires of the Protestant conscience still burn — these people might tear the saints from their niches. The church was crowded with Nellita's multitudinous aunts and cousins — dowdy old people full of kindness and rectitude, and inconspicuous young married couples with well-scrubbed children. The bridesmaids were graceful young girl-cousins, unpowdered and unpainted, with fresh skins and dark eyes full of innocence, sweet seriousness, and malice — like girls in a Russian nineteenth-century novel, but doubtless more Frenchly sensible and their moods controlled by Christian cheerfulness. They wore dark-red dresses made by the village dressmakers and had white narcissus fresh from the garden at Poissy in their hair. The pastor indulged in long extempore prayer (that most hateful of vices). He told the

---

*Nellita McNullty. She married M. Dechaume, a wartime supporter of General de Gaulle.

jeunes mariés that they would *"fonder un foyer — un foyer rayonnant"*. The marriage oath seemed less a solemn abracadabra than a clear promise to break which would be a shame. The thin, clear French language stripped the service of its mystery and beauty and broke the crust of customary acceptance. When the bride and groom answered "Yes", the pastor said: "Que votre 'oui' soit 'oui', car il est donné devant Dieu et Son Eglise." I felt the enormity of lying to God — no fear entered into this feeling, unless it was the fear that one would never forgive oneself.

So in one way and another I had a very amusing time in that last year of bachelordom in Paris. Yet there was an undercurrent of disarray and loneliness. What all that time I wanted, I finally obtained: a happy marriage. I proposed to Sylvia by long-distance telephone, Paris-Ottawa. When she accepted me I knew that this was the greatest stroke of good fortune of my life, and so it has proved to be. Our marriage took place in Ottawa in January 1948 and we returned to Paris until I was posted back to Ottawa in 1950.

May 15,1948
This is a toy house, made for a newly married couple to play in. A pretty eighteenth-century villa of cream-coloured stucco. French windows give from the salon onto a small garden — a square of grass, gravel paths — a Paris garden, without a flower, protected by tall chestnuts from the overlooking windows of the banal blocks of Passy flats. These two or three houses on this side of the street are survivals of an earlier Passy, a quiet suburb merging into the Bois at Auteuil. It is the Passy nostalgically described in the opening pages of du Maurier's *Peter Ibbetson* — a place of old-fashioned peace and gentility. The salon with its corner cupboards full of choice "bits" of china and its

occasional tables has an almost English look of coziness. Our own few things — the framed silhouettes, the plain, worn Georgian silver, even the mid-Victorian water-colour sketch of my grandmother — look at home here. This is much the sort of house they are used to.

Upstairs we are a little cramped for space. The owner of the house, Mlle de Préval, kept the biggest bedroom for herself. Our bed is really too small. It is an old maid's bed, big enough for Mlle de Préval and her hot-water bottle. The window looks out across the roof which projects over the French windows to the garden. At night we hear the trees moving and smell the garden.

Yves seems very well contented. I think he prefers my being married. It means that there is always someone here to take an interest in what he is doing, someone who can measure his successes and failures. Also, he loves entertaining. Tonight, for instance, we are having a dinner party and all day he has been in a state of happy excitement. He is in and out of the house to buy last-moment things — coloured candles for the table (he has a weakness for coloured candles — I hate them), or more flowers. Only now that Sylvia is here she usually buys the flowers herself. She is in the garden now, arranging them in vases for tonight's dinner. She has always been "good with flowers" — I can remember seeing her doing them at Aunt Elsie's house at Murray Bay one summer years ago. I think even then I knew that in the end I should marry her if she would have me.

Thank Heaven they have brought Sylvia's dress for the party. It is a model, borrowed for the night from one of the big couturiers, and has its name inside it on a tab "Quand les lilas refleuriront". It is made of silvery material with a design of lilac branches and has a long train. She will look cool and graceful and flower-like herself. She seems excited herself too — excited and happy. We were going to row on the Lac Inférieur in the Bois today as it is such a gloriously fine May day. For some time she has been wanting to row over to the island in the lake. It looks so tempting, as though the flowers and trees on the island had some magic more than those on the banks beside us when we stand and look across. But all the boats were taken and there was a queue at the landing-place waiting for them to come back to have their turn. There were boats full of young men and girls — the boys stripped to the waist rowing in the sun — people laughing and calling to each other from boat to boat. There were family parties, too — a stout woman sitting in the stern in a black dress and wearing a black hat — a *chétif* little boy dragging his hand in the water — an old man sitting helplessly in the sun-filled boat. You can smell the boats too — the smell, I suppose, of wood — yet it's more than that. It's a smell of *boats*, and even these tame rowboats in a city park have it.

Tonight after dinner we all go on (except the spare man, who is not asked) to an evening party at the British Embassy for Princess Elizabeth. Royalties have an unfortunate effect on any social gathering. No one listens to anything anyone else, or even they themselves, are saying, because they are so anxious to overhear a Royal word or attract a Royal glance.

June 19, 1948

Reading Malraux's *Human Condition*. In it he makes you share his own passion for conspiracy — a passion which has taken possession of some of the bravest, cleverest men in all the countries of Europe and Asia. For this is a conspiratorial age. Power is running in new channels. This is still only true of half of the world, but will that half corrupt the other? Is this one of the clues to what is going on around us? Where there is power there is also conspiracy? Perhaps this has been true in the most respectable parliamentary democracies, but there are conspiracies and conspiracies. What faces us now is something secret, vio-

lent, and fanatical, calling on all the excessive will — the
inhuman, single-track obsession — which can apparently
be found in the most commonplace men. The professor
turned communist — the prostitute turned spy — the
public-school boy turned secret agent. Could this not
become a new form of excitement as necessary to the nerves
as smoking? In France, for instance, everyone has been
plotting in the Resistance, or among the collaborationists,
or just plotting to save their skins or their fortunes, or to
pay off a grudge. They all have been up to something
which had to be concealed. It may be that they have taken
the habit of it. Is a new pattern developing? Is this a
by-product of the omnipotent state? Does it not go on
under ministries where the civil servants increasingly control the lives of nations? Is part of our rage against communism the rage of Caliban at seeing his own face in the glass?

June 21, 1948
Not long ago I was sitting next to Diana at a lively
luncheon party where the cross-fire of conversation was
sizzling away. Twice — three times — I attempted to join
the fray without success. Turning to Diana I said: "I
cannot understand it. Am I invisible, or inaudible? I have
so much to say and no one pays attention to me." She fixed
me with her azure eyes. "Something," she said, "must be
done about that." Something was — with Nancy Mitford
acting as her lieutenant, Diana organized a Ritchie Week,
a week of non-stop parties, dinners, even a ball in Ritchie
honour. She roped in half Paris — surprised French hos-
tesses found it was the smart thing to join in this charade.
Old and new friends showered us with invitations.
Whenever we appeared, a special anthem was played to
signal our entrance. Verses were addressed to us — on the
walls of the houses in our street someone had by night
chalked up in giant letters the slogan "Remember
Ritchie". Nancy I think it was who had an even more

daring inspiration—a clutch of coloured balloons inscribed "Ritchie Week" were let loose over Paris. (The newspapers reported that one of these had floated as far as Boulogne, where it was picked up by the mystified inhabitants, who asked themselves what it might portend.) It was an apotheosis of a kind, and who but Diana could have devised such a fantasy? On the last night of the week, feeling like Cinderella at the end of the ball when she must return to obscurity, I said to Duff, "You don't think, do you, that now we have an *embarras de Ritchies?*" He politely demurred.

June 25, 1948 — in London on a visit

Went to the 400 Club. How often have I sat in that precise corner on the right of the band with the eternal bottle of whisky in front of me and with how many different men and women? Only the bottle has always been the same. Listening to the same band for all these years through the war, and before the war—the hours I have spent in that dark little hole with its dirty silk hangings (actually cleaned now, though not changed) while the rhythm of the monotonous, pointless music, of the drink, of the talk, got into my blood. And always with the thought of what was coming afterwards—the postponing of pleasure which heightened the atmosphere and made one talk more outrageous nonsense. Well, it is quite time I stopped going there. I shall go two or three more times until my present bottle of whisky is finished and then give it up, for to find myself at my age surrounded by boy guardees and their little girlfriends—no—it won't do. It is almost as silly as writing this diary.

July 10, 1948

Everyone in Paris is in a disgruntled temper. You can see it in the faces of the passers-by in the streets, their lips drawn in a line of bad-tempered stoicism. In the Bois the restaurants are empty, a few dejected waiters gossiping among the deserted tables on the terrace. The trees are turning brown as if it were already autumn. Our house is now as dank and dark as a potting-shed. Rain rattles down on the glass of the gallery roof.

In my office I go to the window and look out at the broad, blank spaces of the Avenue Foch. A sour-faced nurse is lugging a reluctant little boy across the grass under the blue-green dripping chestnut trees. Marcel, my chauffeur, has put on his beret and gone to sleep at the wheel of my stationary car. Inside the Embassy everyone seems water-logged with rain, and we roll up and down the grand staircase with no purpose — or a mechanical one.

August 7, 1948

A restless wind — one feels change in the air — brilliant rain-washed intervals, then sudden grey squalls. The house seemed strange. Yves, the man-servant, was away at his son's wedding. The cats, hungry and wild, were snarling at each other and jumping on the tables looking for food. Sylvia, unfamiliar in a blue apron, brought up the breakfast. Later we went for a walk in the Bois — she wore a dress of pale pink linen and her soft-brimmed black hat. People looked at her as if they were saying, "Is she a beauty? No — not really. Oh, wait a minute — perhaps she is."

May 29, 1949

The comedy over the British Embassy Ball for Princess Margaret is worthy of Gogol. First they give out that it is to be for the young people; then it becomes known that they have made a few — a fatal few — exceptions. The fat was immediately in the fire. Men and women are equally frenzied. The men are pretending that they are thinking only of the pleasure their poor, dear wives will miss by not going, or they say, "So far as my wife and I are concerned it is of no consequence. We are too old, I suppose, although no older than the Fordhams" (adding bitterly, "but perhaps we *look* older"). As for the little Princess, she looks a cool little devil with enough in her glance — *maline*, amused, challenging — to turn the boys' heads even if she were not a princess. Neat as a little pin, composed, fresh and dainty in her summer dress with all the Commonwealth and French officials and their wives sweating around her and telling her five hundred times that she has brought the fine weather with her, asking all the right questions with a sweet smile as if butter would not melt in her mouth.

October 16, 1949 — Geneva

It is so long since I have been alone as I have been for the past week in the Hôtel de la Paix. I sit here on this Swiss Sunday morning. Outside my window the lake and the mountains are wrapped in a cocoon of fog. Two disconsolate American businessmen in broad-brimmed fedora hats and granny glasses are walking around the Brunswick Memorial, gazing up at it with hung-over distaste. A Geneva Sunday — everyone wonders whether it was worth waking up at all. I am quite alone up here in my double room (will the Department pay for a *double* room?), thinking that I will drink less, that the barber said that in six months I would be bald, that I am forty-three years old, and in a dim way I like this feeling of being alone and taking up again this monologue. I miss my wife — I want her. I am waiting for her, yet this time of recuperation is quietly, sadly pleasant. If ever I am on the edge of nervous desperation — if ever I feel insanity threatening — I shall buy a ticket for Geneva and come and stay at the Hôtel de la Paix. Geneva is the nursing-home of Europe. Who has not come to rest their bodies and nerves after storms, amorous or political? Every dethroned king, exiled intellectual, proscribed politician in Europe for more than one hundred years. Being alone in Paris is despairing, watching the play of love and fashion, being outside it all, walking the merciless boulevards in the brilliant clarity, hemmed in by the stage-sets of architecture, called on at every turn to respond—to enjoy—to live. Here in Geneva one's forces gather—or one has that illusion; the return attack becomes once more thinkable.

Ottawa

In January 1950 I was posted back to Ottawa from Paris, with the rank of Assistant Under-Secretary of State for External Affairs, and in Ottawa I remained until 1954, becoming Deputy Under-Secretary in 1952 and serving as Acting Under-Secretary for several periods. These years were for me the most satisfying of my professional career. To have reached my rank in the Service gave me a sense of accomplishment. Sharing the management of a government department with all its multifarious problems meant participation in a corporate life and in a corporate loyalty. The Under-Secretary of State for External Affairs, Arnold Heeney, was a great public servant and a warm friend. My colleagues were men and women to whom the job was of exciting importance and to whom hours of work and rates of pay (by no means excessive) meant little compared with the sheer interest of what we were doing. The interest was never lacking, for this was a period in which our country was playing a conspicuous part on the international stage, in NATO, in the United Nations, and in the Commonwealth. In June 1950 the Korean War broke out, and our involvement in it, and the political consequences of the war — in the United Nations, on our relations with the United States, and on our Far Eastern policy — became of dominating importance. During this time I worked closely with our Foreign Minister, Mike Pearson, whom I had known and admired since the war years in London. To be near the operation of power, to live under the tensions of

43

recurrent crises, to participate, in however small a way, in the great game of world politics, all this was immensely stimulating. It also drained away one's other interests, leaving behind it a sediment of dissatisfaction. There was the risk that one's sympathies and amusements with people, one's reaction to the visible world about one, would evaporate, leaving one A Dedicated Civil Servant. The diaries were an escape from this admirable but arid fate. They shut out politics and the office, in an attempt to rediscover an appetite for life.

January 18, 1950 — Ottawa

In winter the town seems to shrink in size without foliage and flowers — the smallness of the plots of garden, the nearness of the houses to each other, become plain — so do the drabness and poverty of the architecture. Snow fills up the spaces and seems to bring the buildings closer together. Ottawa has the look of a sub-Arctic settlement huddled together around the Gothic battlements of the Parliament Buildings. The straggling business streets with their Main Street stores and telegraph poles and the untidy mesh of streetcar wires and telegraph lines look like an old photograph of Ottawa in the 1880s. On a day of blizzard when whirling, skirling snow is blown in gusts around the street corners, when cars are embedded in snowdrifts, and people bent forward against the gale stumble and slide across the snow-piled streets, you feel the isolation of this place as if it had reverted to its early days and was no longer pretending to be a modern capital. The cheerful readiness with which people help each other to dig a car out of the snow has in it something of the original spirit of the pioneer community. Ottawa remains in its soul a small town — not quite like the old, small, settled communities of the East, but more a lumbering settlement in the Ottawa Valley. That spirit still pervades the place.

February 19, 1950

The streets are almost clear of snow — that is to say, the middle of the streets and the pavements — for the snow is banked up in brownish-white piles. It is pre-spring, the season of dirty snow, of mild, melancholy weather, of no-coloured skies. Melting snow drips from the window frames with an uneven drip like a leaking bath-tap. On the roofs of the high buildings men with long poles are dislodging great chunks of ice and masses of half-frozen snow. The streets below are barred off so that these snow-slides should not fall on to the heads of the passing citizenry.

There is the dust that must have lain under the snow on the sidewalks — pale brownish-yellow dust that blows into swirls where the wind catches it at the street corners. It is not worth tidying up the streets, for it will snow again tomorrow and cover the old dropped cigarette packages, car tickets, newspapers which lie in the dust and are blown with it. In this mild air people yawn and stretch and wish for a good skiing snow. The pressure of winter is relaxed — the icy band of cold around forehead and knees, the knife-cutting wind, the brilliance of sun on ice and dazzling white light on the half-frozen snow. This is neither spring nor winter. It will snow again tomorrow.

February 26, 1951

Buffet supper. The men off in the corner talking shop, the women on the sofa talking servants and babies. No sexy flutters or sentimental approaches between men and women. Flat-footed good sense and practical friendliness tinctured by local hates and irritations. Mrs. Griffin told us of an adulterer run out of town by the adulteress's brothers. Four of them went to his hotel bedroom and sat glowering at him with horsewhips in their pockets. Mrs. Griffin approved this manner of dealing with the situation, which she said was "good because it was natural". I said nervously that it sounded like the Wild West. "That's what I mean," she repeated, "it's natural."

Blair Fraser* says we should tell our newly fledged diplomats "No shirt too young to be stuffed".

Easter 1951

Today at Easter communion service I felt boredom, irritation, and then hatred secreting itself in my system. I was surprised by the poisonous strength of these feelings. Where do they come from? The Devil, people once would have said. The Scoutmaster clergyman in the pulpit, the inoffensive congregation, the midday banality of the middle-of-the-way middle-class Church of England morning service goaded me to near hysteria. I felt that I could not take communion in such a state of mind, but when I had taken my place at the altar rail I felt shaken and dissolved, and went back sadly to my pew in the church, not knowing — or caring to know — whether there was God in the bread and wine.

May 21, 1951

It is not the work in the Department that I dislike; in fact, it absorbs me totally. It is the "surround" that goes with it. There is the underlying assumption that anyone who is not overworked, underpaid, eye-strained, joy-starved — in fact, not a senior civil servant — is frivolous or materialistic, that these are the hallmarks of a higher calling, the stigmata of the faithful. "Poor so-and-so, how tired he looks, how overworked," we murmur in tones in which respect mingles with compassion. Why respect? Why not contempt? That a man should so mismanage his life as to be totally immersed in office work is lamentable, unless he loves it. If he loves it, he is doing what he wants,

*Blair Fraser, the Canadian journalist, was an old friend.

like another who drinks himself to a standstill, and he has no particular call on our sympathy. A civilized, curious, pleasure- and thought-loving man, reduced to a dreary, weary automaton. What is there to respect in that painful spectacle?

May 23, 1951

The subject I should like to write about is love between brother and sister, growing up together as children in an old house with their grandfather and a couple of aunts, his daughters. They would be orphans, and the boy would be raised on stories of their picturesque or dashing father killed in the war, and their mother who died when the boy was born. As their lives went on they would discover that no man or woman could satisfy them, that the bond between them was so strong that it unfitted them for any other love and made them destructive in love. Entangled with this subject is another, that of the personality of the dead father as interpreted in the old wives' tales of the aunts, acting upon the boy as an influence so much stronger than that of any living person and building his naturally timid nature into rash, would-be-heroic shapes.

Well, back to this diary again. If I must do it, let me make my little messes in private. God knows who will clean them up after I am gone. I hope someone who will not be bored by them. It would be appalling to be a Bore after one was dead — an immortal Bore.

"All the spring goes on without her" — where does that come from? This Ottawa spring is beautiful, but they can have it. I find it quite an effort to remember that this life is real — that it matters whether you do up your fly before going out in the street, or call people by their right names. Only in the office I mean business. Otherwise, there is the habit of not hurting people's feelings, of being on time for dinner, of having three large whiskies between six and eight, and of being a little uneasy about money.

July 2, 1951 — Wolfville, Nova Scotia, on vacation

I feel as if I were recuperating after a serious illness. Outside it is perfect June weather — sunlight on a white house — on a slope of neighbouring lawn. The main street is almost deserted at this midday hour. At Frank's Clothing Store the removal sale is slowing down. At Babcock's Restaurant and Soda Fountain Mr. and Mrs. Babcock and the two waitresses are recovering after the rush of the Dominion Day crowds. The Post Office is empty — people collected their mail at the bustling hour of twelve after the Halifax train had come in. In the old-fashioned frame houses behind the roomy porches and the standard rose-bushes, sundry old ladies are resting — resting their rheumatism, their weak hearts, their jangled nerves. The little church on the bluff overlooking Minas Basin is cool, dark, and empty. Light comes through the Sherwood memorial window in crimson-lake puddles. In the church-yard the de Wolfs — the town's founders — lie. From the grassy ledge at the verge of the cliff where the churchyard ends abruptly I can see the whole curve of the land round the water of Minas Basin. The tide is in now, right up to the edge of the dykes and in places seeping through into the dyke land that lies directly below me. Beyond the picture-postcard blue of the water rises Blomidon, swathed in a hyacinth mist, drawing the eye and the imagination — that sombre and dramatic shape dominates the seascapes of mist and water and the receding mauve folds of hills that lie behind it. I am half bored, half enchanted, by this long stretch of June days, by the hot, sweet smells of clover fields, of wild-strawberry patches, the breeze off the water that always keeps the tall elm trees stirring and that blows pollen from flowering bushes in tenderly tended cottage gardens. In and out of the sunny main street too blows the town's gossip — blowing like pollen from house to house, from garden to garden.

November 11, 1951 — Ottawa

Sunday afternoon again. A grey, dank, damp day — old tin cans lying in dirty slush in the gutters. I walked in from Rockcliffe across the bridge over the grey river which is slowing to freezing-point. The hills, the Laurentians, glow like dark sapphires. Somewhere around the corner a band was playing and soldiers marching back from the Armistice ceremonies. Plump, bright-eyed French-Canadian girls were strolling with their boyfriends through the dirty streets; French-Canadian mothers-of-ten were taking their brood for a Sunday walk, accompanied by their husbands. Rounding the corner by the Château Laurier to go up to my office I thought how very much I should prefer to find myself in a big double bed making love.

November 27, 1951

Aunt Beatrice came to dinner tonight — eighty-four — recently (three weeks) widowed, just flown out to Canada after fifty years of county life in Northern Ireland. She sits in her black and pearls, talking about Dundarave, the place which the law of entail has obliged her to quit in favour of an unworthy nephew, and of the follies of the housemaids. She is a plucky old girl with spirit and stoicism. I like it when she talks about her niece being "so good at cartooms — always been artistic". After dinner we looked at old photographs with her — those embalmed moments of lightheartedness at picnics when the men put their straw hats on back to front or enacted facetious courtship scenes with the girls before the camera in the sunlit summer of 1900. How depressing it is to look through these albums now with a survivor of the picnics, skating parties, and weekend gaieties. There is no physical connection, not the slightest, between that laughing girl in the canoe with the towering flowered hat, the tie and

starched shirt, and the old woman beside me. "Look,"
Beatrice says, "at the clothes. How could we have worn
them? The hats, my dear, such a suitable outfit to go
canoeing in! I was considered very fast for wearing a soft
collar to play tennis in. An older married woman told me,
'Of course there is nothing wrong in it, but I should wear a
stiff collar in future if you don't want to get the reputation
of being a fast girl.' " Those three sisters* must have been
quite a feature of Ottawa in those days, with quick wits, a
great sense of fun, and no money, but determined to be in
on everything. Endless flirtations, Beatrice's courtship by
Lord Ava—"he wrote me the only real love letter, what
you would call a love letter, that I have ever had. The
best-looking man I ever knew. Died at Ladysmith in the
South African war." And Harold, who proposed to all
three sisters, and whose daily letters, lying on the radiator
in the hall, were greeted by the other sisters with "Elsie,
the daily question is waiting for you on the marble slab."
Why do I write about these old sisters? I spend my days
with Cabinet Ministers, distinguished (and interesting)
civil servants—I am in a good position to report the gossip
and politics of society in this little but important place,
but

> I have old women's secrets now
> That had those of the young;
> Madge tells me what I dared not think
> When my blood was strong,
> And what had drowned a lover once
> Sounds like an old song.   (*W.B. Yeats*)

When I was young I used to be shocked by the callousness
of the old, the casual way they would look at a photograph

---

*The three sisters, daughters of Sir William Ritchie, Chief Justice of
Canada, were: Beatrice, Lady Macnaghten; Elsie, Mrs. W. H. Rowley
(mother of John and Roger Rowley); and Amy, Mrs. James Smellie (mother of
my wife, Sylvia, and her brother, Peter Smellie).

and say, "She used to be my closest friend. She was so pretty and gay. She married a very ordinary man in Toronto and I don't know what happened to her in the end." I expected, somehow, more feeling, a pause to think of years of friendship, the tragedy of change, the decline of everything — including themselves. Now I think that Proust's ruthless analysis of old age is not cynical but the simple truth — as the capacity for feeling shrinks, as the freshness of interests narrows, brain and heart contract. I fear it in myself. Or perhaps feeling becomes more canalized — there is less overflow. Two or three human beings out of one's whole world of people seem the only ones truly human.

March 20, 1952

From the world into which I was born, cruelty, violence, and coarseness were altogether excluded. Pain, and even discomfort, were fended off wherever possible. Apprehensions of illness were always in the air, perhaps because illness seemed the only enemy likely to penetrate the defences of my home. Security was — or seemed — complete in those days before 1914 as it has never seemed since. Security in this world and the next, for my parents' generation was the first to retain a belief in Heaven while dispensing with the fear of Hell. It was felt that Hell was a Victorian superstition. Since God was Love and it was unthinkable that he would punish His children with perpetual torment, it would be wrong to darken a child's mind with such horrors. Hell might exist for some unspeakable outsiders, but in any case, like sex, it was not to be mentioned before children.

A sub-fusc day, grey sky dripping on dirty snow. Spring in Ottawa is not a season but one vast mopping-up operation. Civil servants, glum or smug, have now — at 9.30 — been absorbed into the government buildings. The whole population seems mewed up, like the animals in the

Ark. The Parliament Buildings, like the Ark, ride high above the surrounding slush and puddle. Silence reigns in the dripping and now almost empty streets. Stenographers are now adjusting in their typewriters the first memorandum (with carbon copy) of this day; their bosses, with or without hangovers, are girding themselves for the day's effort to get nearer the top of their grade. In their homes the wireless whines and housewives prepare lists of purchases for Steinberg's and the A & P. The melting ice discloses an old overshoe, or a French safe, buried throughout the winter under the snow — our Ottawa version of the spring crocus.

This last week has flashed by in days of high-pressure work, absorbed in this absorbing little world where politics and diplomacy merge into personalities. You spend the day working with this group of politicians, officials, and diplomats, then you dine with them and their wives, gossip with them, and drink with them. The dominant theme — the only point in this place — is the pursuit of power. It obsesses the men and infects the women. Other societies may be dominated by money, snobbery, or the search for pleasure. Here the game of political power is the only one that really counts. It creates an atmosphere very uncongenial to love, very unflattering to women — almost any man in official Ottawa would rather talk to a Cabinet Minister than to the most beautiful woman in the room. It is easy to understand this once you are inside the game. You are tuned in to the power waves and you can hardly hear any others, except as "interference". This is the game for middle-aged men — you can even play it into the sixties or seventies with growing expertise, when you would be at a sad disadvantage in the games of love.

June 17, 1952 — Wolfville, Nova Scotia
I am here on a visit with my mother. The road into Wolfville runs parallel to the shoreline of Minas Basin.

You only see the broad stretch of water and the bold profile of Blomidon at intervals. Most of the time it is blotted out by fields and houses, but even the unseen presence of that magic mountain makes the banality of the main street seem reassuring and cozy. The little town seems like a place met with at the very beginning of a fairy story, before out-of-the-way things start happening — a jumping-off place and a place to which, in the end, one is not sorry to return, to see its lights cheerfully glowing after an excursion into strange terrain.

August 31, 1952 — Ottawa

Last night after dinner we went out into the street to watch the Northern Lights. I have never seen them in such magnificence. Anyone who did not choose to call them Northern Lights could not fail to think that this was a revelation of God, his power moving in the firmament; the long, quivering fingers of light seemed alive as they wove their shifting patterns in the sky. At one moment a cone of light at the top of the sky seemed to shed just those rays seen in sacred pictures, and one could expect a Blake-like vision of God the Father. The silent shiftings of these long cones of light and the subtle, swift sliding of one colour into another seemed a performance of intricate music, a manifestation of a vast, benign, and playful intelligence — the music of the spheres. And then suddenly it became for me a most unbearable bore. I went into the house and deliberately picked up a novel and read it, to escape the imposition of sublimity. I felt the same kind of sleepiness, restlessness, and revolt which great music, mountain peaks, and sunsets produce after a brief exaltation in me.

December 6, 1952
   Work.

December 7, 1952
   Work.

December 8, 1952
    Work.

December 9, 1952
    Work.

December 10, 1952
    I am now in charge of the Department of External Affairs.

January, 1953
    Work, work, work.

    One day in the autumn of 1953 I told the Minister, Mike Pearson, that I wanted to be posted abroad. He was reproachful and urged me to stay, saying, "I thought you were a *working* diplomat and did not care for a representational job." He was quite right — I was never to enjoy the representative side of an ambassador's role and always to look back upon my days in the Department as the most satisfying of my career. But once my decision was taken I could not wait to go, and I used to fear that I might break a leg on the icy streets of Ottawa and have my departure delayed. With this onset of restlessness came a return to the diaries.

October 7, 1953 — Ottawa
    This last weekend was warm enough to come up to the Wrongs'* cottage in the Gatineau country outside Ottawa. Yet it is hardly warm enough. We had to huddle before a fire last night but today it has turned to this soft, fickle weather, with warm days on sheltered wharves by the lake with the sun on them but, high up here on the verandah, a chilly wind blowing across the lake. Sylvia, at the other end of the verandah, is painting my portrait. She

---

*Hume Wrong, Canadian Ambassador to Washington and Under-Secretary of State for External Affairs, and his wife, Joyce.

has me writing, clad in a blue dressing-gown, and has made me look like Harold Laski, my least favourite character.

It is very quiet here except for the wind in the pines around the house, the sound of cowbells from the farm near by where we get water in pails, and the occasional cars passing on the nearby road. The house is full of brown and red butterflies, the colour of the changing leaves. They crawl against the mosquito netting on the verandah, trying to get out. I pick them up very delicately between finger and thumb by their closed wings, open the screen door, and throw them into the air. The verandah floor is strewn with obsolescent wasps, torpid in this autumn air with hardly the spirit left to sting.

The signs are for a peculiar season. Squirrels are making no hoards of nuts; there are no berries on the trees. The bears, driven out of the woods by the forest fires, have come as near as the suburbs. It is too warm for them to hibernate and they go blundering round outlying farms, beating down barn doors in search of food, in an ugly mood, put out of their annual routine.

For my part, like the animals I feel a break in routine. I am once again on the edge of one of those trans-Atlantic migrations which have been the pattern of my life. I am going back to Europe, away from the mindless beauty of these woods and lakes, away from the daily reassurance of making good in a community where there is no attractive way of going to the bad. One fact about Ottawa has from the first been clear — that for me there is only one temptation here, whisky. How often have I vowed that whatever else this place does to me it is not going to make me into a drunk.

October 23, 1953

There go those Sunday bells from the carillon of the Peace Tower of the Parliament Buildings! I can never forgive Ottawa its Sundays, yet I am conditioned to this

place and to the work in the office and am somehow scared
of a change and of being turned back on my own resources
after the incessant work of the office. It is only a few weeks
now before I leave for England and then to accompany the
Prime Minister on his tour of the Far East and after that,
God knows what. They have suggested my going as
Ambassador to Madrid but I cannot face it. There is no
work there and one could not live on picturesque views of
Spain and visits to the Prado.

This job as Deputy Under-Secretary for External
Affairs has been a tough one, requiring toughness in the
occupant. It also needs experience. On top of that, it calls
for a certain flair for sensing the situation and subjects
which are "sensitive", in which a mistake can rapidly
become a blunder. I have the experience and something of
the flair, but I lack the toughness.

So far as policy is in question, I see policy as a balance,
also a calculated risk, as the tortuous approach to an
ill-defined objective. All-out decisions, unqualified statements, irreconcilable antagonisms are foreign to my
nature and to my training. In these ways I reflect my
political masters, the inheritors of Mackenzie King, and I
am fitted to work with them. I believe, too, that such
temperaments are needed in this dangerous period of history, which is no time for heroics to be paid for in a
currency of disaster.

In administration I tend to the concrete and the
human and want to break the rules to fit the individual
case, the object to get out of people the most effective
element that they can contribute. This may lead to injus-
tice but would avoid the worse thing — waste. My ignorance of and contempt for rules and regulations would
wreck any system unless counterbalanced by someone who
could sustain the necessary framework. But most of the
time I am simply rushed off my feet with work, passing by
human situations which would be obvious if I had the time

to look twice, making decisions by a mixture of know-how and instinct, always in danger of a mistake or a lost opportunity or a damaging delay.

December 13, 1953
It is Jack Pickersgill, always a good friend to me and very close to the Prime Minister, who has suggested my name to Mr. St. Laurent to accompany him on his visit to Europe and the Far East. I am to be his External Affairs adviser, to accompany him on his official calls on prime ministers and heads of state, to keep a record of his conversations with them, and generally to make myself useful. I approach this assignment with trepidation. I do not know Mr. St. Laurent or how I shall get on with him. Also, I do not know the Far East and am nervous lest he pepper me with questions about these countries to which I cannot supply the answers. His daughter Madeleine, his son Jean-Paul, are going with him, plus a small entourage including a doctor, his secretary — the admirable Annette Perron, the clever and charming young Ross Martin from the Privy Council Office, on whom I shall depend a lot for companionship, and an elderly and none-too-efficient valet. We shall fly all the way in an RCAF plane whose captain, John Stevenson, I have just met. He is handsome, humorous, and, I should think, eminently capable.

I intend to try to keep up this diary during the trip but the official and political record will be contained in the telegrams which I shall be drafting for the Prime Minister's approval, so that this will be a matter of personal impressions.

It is to be a tour of goodwill, support, and friendship and no concrete results are expected.

February 12, 1954 — Bonn
This is the first moment that I have been able to catch my breath for long enough to return to this diary. We have

just arrived here from the Prime Minister's visit to Paris, which, from the political point of view, I found deeply depressing. I have been drafting the telegrams giving the high points of the Prime Minister's interviews with M. Schuman and the other political leaders. Their general outlook on the world was one of profound anxiety and negativism. There was no belief in the European Defence Community in its present form and they had no suggestions for alternatives.

The Prime Minister, his daughter Madeleine, and I stayed at our Embassy, which is a magnificent house in the rue du Faubourg Saint-Honoré. The visit got off on the wrong foot from the start. From the moment that we entered the panelled salon with its chandeliers and elegant eighteenth-century furniture, with a footman bringing glasses of champagne on a silver salver, I could see that the Prime Minister, who was tired anyway, did not at all appreciate this style of "gracious living" (which I know he thinks is "un-Canadian"). The Ambassadress, the beautiful Madame Désy, did not help matters. Encased in satin, she seemed frozen into a formal attitude like an ambassadress in a play. Jean Désy talked with nervous intensity. He is a highly intelligent man but should have sensed that the Prime Minister was not in a responsive mood.

Dinner was even worse. We filed into the beautiful but chilly Louis Seize dining-room and were spaced at wide intervals round a marble table. The food was elaborate, the wines varied, the conversation stilted in the extreme. At times there were pools of silence of several moments' duration. For some reason, and although I was not in any way responsible for the social freeze, I began myself to feel both nervous and embarrassed. I do not know whether it was cause and effect, but, biting on a piece of toast Melba, a loose tooth suddenly came unstuck, falling into my cup of consommé with a plop which was clearly audible in the silence round the table and drew all eyes upon me.

February 15, 1954 — Bonn

The contrast in political atmosphere between this place and Paris is extraordinary. There is no mistaking the ability and forcefulness of the German government *équipe*, and owing to the smaller scale of the entertainments offered us we have been able to meet and talk to them on a much more intimate and informal basis than in Paris. Here we encountered a firmness of policy line, energy, and decisiveness. Bonn is a deceptive place, in appearance a sleepy university town, but there is an impression of underlying German dynamism and potential strength. To anyone who, like myself, would prefer to see the French in command of the destinies of Western Europe, this is not altogether reassuring.

The Prime Minister's interview with Chancellor Adenauer went well. I should say, fairly well. Mr. St. Laurent seemed a little disconcerted by Adenauer's cynical outspokenness about international personalities and policies. Our man, no doubt wisely, refused to be drawn and restricted himself to expressions of goodwill and careful platitudes, of which, I must say, he has a steady stock. I was much impressed by Adenauer. There is something very formidable about him. He is like a well-oiled, immensely powerful machine moving in the groove. He emanates authority and an unmistakable *Catholic* touch. His assessments of international forces were realistic. He is adroit, patient, and ironic. His mobility of gait and gesture combine with the mask-like pallor of his face (reconstructed after a motor accident) to leave an impression of agelessness almost uncanny in a man of seventy-six, or is it seventy-eight?

February 16, 1954 — Rome

The Italian government is new in office, and insecure. The conversations with Italian politicians have been flimsy indeed; the hospitality on a splendid scale.

Our ambassador here is my old friend Pierre Dupuy,

witty, intelligent, one of our best diplomats. There was a funny scene between him and the Prime Minister over the vexed question of exchange of gifts with the Italian government. The Italians have presented the Prime Minister with something handsome in the line of silver and Pierre demurred at the Prime Minister's intention to reciprocate with a signed photograph in a frame which was not even leather but leatherette, and cheap-looking at that. Pierre pleaded for a silver frame, saying "Prime Minister, in Rome do as the Romans do," to which the Prime Minister drily replied, "In Rome *we* do as Canadians do."

The Prime Minister has handled himself throughout these meetings with European political leaders with good sense and dignity, and without pomposity. His charm and warmth and his distinguished appearance are attractive. As a Canadian, one feels proud of him, which is more than I can say for all our travelling Canadian politicians. Madeleine is a great asset. Beautiful to look at, spontaneous and friendly and with a sense of humour. She and her father share a dislike of artificiality and pretence.

The Prime Minister has kept to a line in all his interviews: (1) he has emphasized NATO bonds but refrained from any particular proposal in the NATO framework; (2) he has used the analogy of relations between people of English and French stock in Canada to show how it is possible to cure ancient rivalries and live in productive and friendly relations; (3) he has conveyed throughout that it is enlightened self-interest that has guided Canada in entering into defensive arrangements and in her immigration and trade policies — a frankness which has been appreciated by European statesmen who are a little tired of lofty moral sentiments which conceal interested motives; (4) in his assessment of the risk of war he has expressed his judgement that the U.S.S.R. does not intend war but wants to maintain tension, and this necessitates continued preparedness. On this point there has been striking unanimity among all European statesmen. None believed that aggressive war would be launched by the Russians; none believed in the possibility at this time of a settled peace.

February 17, 1954 — Bahrein

Bahrein is flooded. They have had rains here such as never before in their history. But today is a fine day, cool after the rain, a stiff breeze on the sea front. Veiled Arab women pick their way across the flooded streets on stepping-stones. In his hovel shop a bearded and turbaned sage smoking a hookah sells you Gillette blades and Colgate toothpaste. The bar of the BOAC hotel is full of types who seem to be deliberately playing up their parts. The manager, ex-RAF, says, "Franco nearly got me in the civil war. I was one of the bad boys in the International Brigade — born on the Khyber Pass — ask them up there if they remember Cook Sahib. That was my old man." A Danish sea-captain, washed up here because the Japanese took over his ship, describes life in Bahrein: "You wait till the bar opens, drink till lunch, sleep, wait till the bar opens, and drink till dinner, then just drink."

February 20, 1954 — Peshawar

Seldom have I come to a place which has had the same instant attraction for me as this. County Cork, the town of Avalon in France, the Isle of Jura, Wolfville in Nova Scotia — all were cases of love at first sight for me. When I awoke this morning it was to hear the Moslem call to prayer floating over an English garden. We are staying at the local Government House. From my window I see an English vista, a village church, hedges, English trees, a cricket ground. The call to prayer and the sound of command and of the bugle are always in the air in Pakistan, yet there is something peculiar to Peshawar, as if we were staying in someone's house when the host was away. The English haunt the place.

February 21, 1954

Up the Khyber Pass. Almost too good to be true, the exhilarating air, the sense of plunging straight into a boy's adventure story — the tough, hard-drinking commander of the Border Scouts whose idea of fun is to stir up a scrap with the Afghans, an atmosphere of virility, adventure, keen air, dramatic heights with the solitary figure of a Khyber Scout perched on a rock guarding the path against the fighting tribesmen with their home-made guns. The sense of adventure, for us at any rate, was spurious. The Pass is perfectly safe now and in another five years will be placarded with Pepsodent advertisements. But cut into the rocks are the emblems of the regiments, British and Indian, who fought in this wild country. The biggest danger I encountered was from the Pakistani colleague who sat in the car next to me sneezing virulently at me as if on purpose till finally I have caught his cold.

On to Lahore. Our knowledge of the subcontinent appears to be restricted to Government Houses. The Government House in Lahore is a cream-coloured, pillared, sprawling mansion, brilliant in sunlight. The bookshelves are filled with out-of-date English novels (many W. J. Lockes) and old sepia-tinted photographs of picnics and polo games. There is tea before breakfast, the bath is drawn. The servants never leave one alone for an instant. An individual bottle of whisky is brought to one's room to prepare one for the interminable Moslem banquets without a drop but water to drink. These drinkless banquets and the endless polite conversation are pretty exhausting. Last evening I went in company with a supercilious maharanee and members of the local smart set to the ball for the end of the Lahore horse show. I might as well have been in the Golf Club in Ottawa — the same kind of talk, the same tunes from the band, but with Moslem ladies sitting in groups, not dancing.

February 24, 1954 — New Delhi

From the moment that we arrived at the New Delhi airport we were in a different world from Pakistan — more settled, richer, neater, less of a poor, untidy pioneer country. The contrast between Karachi and New Delhi is overwhelming. Here is a garden city of broad streets and houses set back among green gardens. No refugees, as in Pakistan, no squalor, no stink, modern cars glide over the asphalt. Here the Foreign Office is a fine stone building, solid and gleamingly clean. I thought of the Karachi Foreign Office in the dilapidated Rajah's Palace, open to the sandstorms, untidy, improvised like everything in Karachi. And how different are the people. The Moslems in Karachi seemed straightforward, frank, simple, compared with the alien sophistication of the Hindu, a strangeness lurking just under the surface of the Oxford-educated civil servants with whom we associate. Then there is the mixture of morality and the Machiavellian in their politics, their vanity and subtlety in social relations, the insinuating intelligence, the charm which might just be disconcerting.

We are staying in what used to be the Viceroy's house here, Lutyens' palace, imposing, original, monumental, and monumentally successful, an establishment on the scale of Versailles. Indeed, Versailles in its pompous emphasis is the only palace comparable to this. Hundreds of servants, hundreds of gardeners, hundreds of cooks in the kitchen (I believe there are eight hundred servants in all). Some are turbaned; some, in a curious livery of scarlet and gold, wear flat Chinese hats. A turbaned, bearded father-figure brings in breakfast and stands over you while you eat it. The bath-tubs are of marble, built for giants. In the interminable marble halls are yet other attendants who hover and cluster and come bowing forward to put you in one of the lifts which never, to their great chagrin, can they move without a hitch from one floor to another. In the great courtyard standing under every arch, patrolling the mogul garden, are the soldiers of the Government House bodyguard.

The Prime Minister had been looking forward to this visit and his meeting with Nehru as the high point of his tour. He and Nehru have been conducting a tremendous pen-pal friendship for months. They have been exchanging interminable telegrams of mutual congratulation and esteem, but I am not at all sure how this love affair is going to prosper. It was surprising to Mr. St. Laurent to find that this Wise Man of the East conversed in the style and language of Bloomsbury, a style very far from the Prime Minister's own. However, our High Commissioner here, Escott Reid, seems to think that the talks between them, after a shaky start, are going extremely well. I have not been present at their official meetings, as Escott has taken over. If anyone can make the visit a success Escott can, as in addition to his exceptional ability and charm of manner he is an enthusiastic lover of India.

As for one's impression of Nehru, what can one say? The English painter who has come out here to paint his portrait says that the task is impossible. A thousand expressions flicker across his face. When he met us at the airport he jumped about from one foot to the other, making the gesture of pulling up his long white cotton trousers as if they were slipping down. He kept twisting the red rose in the buttonhole of his long cream-coloured linen coat, and made as if to scratch the top of his white Gandhi hat. He is always in movement, never still, or if he is, his eyes are always moving, or his mouth. He is not the pontifical figure I had expected. Gayer, more mobile, more immediate; impatient, too, between a caress and a barb.

Last night we dined with him — the Prime Minister, Madeleine, and myself. It is, I think, unfortunate from the point of view of a *"prise de contact"* between him and Mr. St. Laurent that Lady Mountbatten should be staying here. She strikes a Mayfair note which the Prime Minister cannot pick up. When we arrived in the hall of Mr. Nehru's house it was she who greeted us, looking charming yet lined and wrinkled from gracious smiling. In the hall was a head of Nehru by Epstein. The Prime Minister remarked, "Well, I suppose that is a very fine likeness." Lady Mountbatten emitted a little cry of horror and said, "Oh, don't tell *him* that. It is too ghastly and must be got rid of." The Prime Minister looked somewhat at a loss.

At dinner there was no real opportunity for any consecutive talk between the two men. After dinner, long pauses in the conversation began to set in. Finally Lady Mountbatten, to break the log-jam, said to Nehru, "Do show the Prime Minister your Tibetan costume and your Kashmiri dressing-gown." At once Nehru jumped to his feet and, slightly stooped, ran from the room. (We do not move as these people do or run in this sudden, lightfooted way.) After a longish interval he returned, clad in a magnificent Kashmiri dressing-gown, then disappeared again, to return in Tibetan dress. He seemed to be much enjoying himself and relieved to escape from conversational effort.

February 27, 1954 — Viceroy's House, New Delhi
I have taken to my bed with some kind of throat infection. Outside my window in the darkening dusk the great raised courtyard looks like a stage-set. Any figure appearing there has significance. After a day of silence, at evening there is a monkey chatter of talk from the soldiers

below who have come off duty. The flowers in my "sick room" — sweet peas and phlox — have no scent. Perhaps no English flowers smell here.

Last night was Mr. Nehru's dinner in honour of the Prime Minister — white tie and decorations (if any). At the hour of dinner I had a call to go to the Prime Minister's bedroom. I found him standing in the middle of the room, white tie, white waistcoat, tailcoat, long woollen underwear, no trousers. He said, "Here now, I suppose my trousers have been left on the plane." That was precisely what had happened. Everyone else in his entourage had his trousers, but the Prime Minister was trouserless. Like Sir Walter Raleigh throwing down his cloak for Queen Elizabeth to walk upon, I said, "Take mine, Prime Minister," but a second look at his girth and mine showed that this was a physical impossibility. I called one of the innumerable servants to inquire after a pair of spare trousers, but apparently there are none in this vast palace. We sent him running to the nearest bazaar in New Delhi to purchase a pair. The moments ticked by. The Prime Minister was already eleven minutes late for dinner. Finally the servant returned bearing with him an extremely greasy pair of second- or third-hand trousers of such circumference that they had to be fastened round the Prime Minister's waist with safety-pins. During the whole of this agonizing ordeal Mr. St. Laurent remained perfectly unperturbed and patient, with never a word of complaint. My mind boggled at the thought of what Mackenzie King would have said in these circumstances.

Finally we descended to dinner. Turbaned Lancers behind every chair, magnificent flowers on the table, no wine. During the endless dinner party three pigeons flew into the dining-room from the garden through the French windows and perched on the cornice above the fireplace. They behaved very well for quite a long time until boredom with the after-dinner speeches drove them to fly high

across the long candle-lit table with protesting cries and
out of the windows again.

During the Prime Minister's speech before the
Assembly the Indians only applauded the compliments to
themselves. I don't believe that, apart from the meetings
with political leaders, anything we have said or done on
this visit has got across to the minds or hearts of these
people. They are easily bored and I think that they have
been.

The sentiment heard in government circles is
extremely anti-American. The Americans can do no right
in Indian eyes. At one moment they are accused of selfish
isolationism and neglect of poorer countries, at the next of
imperialist ambitions to dominate. There is a great deal of
harping on American materialism in contrast to the
spiritual values of India. I am beginning to find this very
irritating. As a Canadian, I feel quite free to criticize the
Americans, but when other people do it I instinctively
rally to their defence.

I had a long talk the day before yesterday at one of
these endless lemonade-drinking receptions with Indira,
Nehru's daughter. She is a handsome woman, but cold.
She talked humanitarianism and social reform but in a
bloodless fashion, tinged with immense smugness and
self-righteousness. I took strongly against her.

A day of sight-seeing. Fatehpur Sikri in the morning.
Talk of a deserted Mogul capital had put me on the wrong
track. I had expected romantic ruins. What I found was a
creation of art so totally new to me that it might have been
new in time. The completeness, the state of preservation,
are due to the accident of its being abandoned by Akbar
and thus never plundered or destroyed by armies. Those
courtyards, mosques, and pavilions of red sandstone are
unhaunted, picked dry of all human context by the heat of
the sun. Or is it simply the advantage of my ignorance that
I can see these monuments as timeless works of art because

I do not know the language of their history which would set them safely in a framework?

The Prime Minister said that he pictured in his imagination the carpets and fountains of the time of the Mogul court. He responds to every impression in India. He seems as interested in ancient monuments as he is in pipelines and the complexities of corporation law. I find it very attractive that a man of his age and in his position should be so open to new impressions. He says that never in his life has he had such a sense of new experience as in this one week in India. Perhaps it is doing the same thing for him as it is doing for me. Yet how profoundly alien India is; nothing responds to my predilections. I do not "love" this country, I am not even "attracted" to it, but I feel it is a multitudinous sea in which one might shed one's personality.

February 28, 1954 — Colombo

When we got here last night, Madeleine stretched back in her chair and, kicking off her shoes, said, "Well, I guess I like the small countries." We all knew what she meant. The complexity and sophistication of India, the grandeur of its monuments, the imperial touch, Mogul or British, all imposed their strain. Canadians cannot quite stomach the excessive. Then, too, we are beginning to tire. From Government House to Government House, from dinner party to dinner party, from reception to reception, from interview to interview, from Bombay to Madras. Ceylon seems a holiday after India. The friendliness of the people, the disorganization at the airport. It is a spice island of flowers and fruits and voluptuous foliage.

March 8, 1954 — Ottawa

After Ceylon I gave up keeping this diary. Some day I shall try to sort out my impressions of the rest of the trip. At the moment they're a jumble of unrelated details.

Jakarta, with Sukarno boasting and posturing; the squalor of war-wrecked Seoul, bad oysters at dinner with horrible old Syngman Rhee, the visit to the Canadian troops at the front in Korea; Tokyo and lunch with the Emperor, where two silences met, the silence of the Prime Minister and the even more extensive silence of Emperor Hirohito, blinking through his thick-lensed glasses; the pointless visit to Manila.

It was at Tokyo that the Prime Minister began to show signs of fatigue. From being tired he began to show signs of melancholy. He seemed austere and more abrupt. I am beginning to fear that this trip has been too much for him.

Honolulu is a boring place, Hawaiian music sick-making. They hung leis of flowers round our necks at the airport, making us — apart from Madeleine — look extremely silly. In my bedroom at the Royal Hawaiian Hotel was a pineapple with a card "Compliments of the Manager". The pineapple was already sliced. I thought it looked delicious and went out for a brief walk, intending to eat some of it on my return. When I got back it had gone. I telephoned the room service and asked, "Where is my pineapple with the Manager's compliments?" "Aloha," a voice replied (they always say "Aloha" in Honolulu instead of "Hallo"). "Aloha, pineapples only left in rooms to welcome guests on arrival." I never saw that pineapple again.

March 10, 1954 — Ottawa
Ever since I got back I have been working on the draft of a speech for the Prime Minister to make in the House of Commons about his tour. It was not an easy job but after about eight drafts I felt reasonably satisfied with it. The Prime Minister read it and then said, "Here now, Charles, I suppose you have told me what I *don't* want to say." Rather nettled, I replied, "Prime Minister, I am glad to

have been able to clarify your thinking." I went to the gallery of the House of Commons to listen to the Prime Minister deliver *his* version of the speech, which I found absolutely deplorable.

Looking back on my association with Mr. St. Laurent during the trip, I think that though he treated me with so much kindness and consulted me so frequently, I am no closer to him than I was at the outset. As Norman Robertson* said of his own relationship with Mr. St. Laurent, "Our natures and our minds do not mesh." Yet I respect him, I admire him, and I could be fond of him if personal relations meant anything to him, which I think they do not, apart from his devotion to his family. His philosophy of life seems to be a sort of Roman Catholic Rotarianism which does not admit the existence of evil. He lives by Christian rule. I have never heard him say an uncharitable thing. Also, he never praises. His mind is more a lawyer's mind than a politician's, and he is completely free from the vanity and the grudges of political life, hates gossip, does not drink, has great public charm, no small talk, humour *très sec*.

April 6, 1954 — Amherst, Nova Scotia

My mother and I are here on a visit for a few days. The wind never stops blowing in from the Tantramar marshes. Only the eye of love could descry beauty in Amherst. It is fascinating to see how different each of these Nova Scotian small towns is from the other. Wolfville is charming, indeed pretty, the houses painted in spotless white, the gardens tended, trees surrounding the colonial houses. Much of Amherst dates from about 1880 when it was "busy Amherst", a boom industrial village-town, now in decline. It is not helped by the unhappy attraction that a kind of maroon sandstone had for Amherst builders and of

---

*Norman A. Robertson, twice Under-Secretary of State for External Affairs, Ambassador to Washington, and High Commissioner to London.

which many of the buildings, including the post office and the Baptist church in the main street, are built.

The town is at the edge of the marshes, which gives it something of the character of a seaside place. The streets all end abruptly where the marsh begins. Beyond is space and skyscape. An eternal wind blows from those marshes. Yes, it is a peculiar little town.

My mother's family came from here. The only traces left of them are the stained-glass windows (ordered out from England) in the little Anglican church, and the graves on the windy marsh side — "The Honourable Alexander Stewart, C.B., Master of the Rolls" and his children and his grandchildren. In the church there is a brass to the last man in the family, my mother's brother, "Lt.-Colonel Charles James Townshend Stewart, D.S.O., Croix de Guerre, killed in action Bourlon Wood, October 20, 1918". No one in Amherst even remembers the Stewart name now, yet the old man aspired to Found a Family only a hundred years ago and we still live on what is left of his money. We are children or grandchildren of the small town and have never quite got free of its influence. Those dire words, "What will the neighbours say?" still echo in the ears on a hung-over morning.

April 21, 1954 — Ottawa

In two weeks' time I leave to take up my appointment as Ambassador to Bonn and Head of the Military Mission in Berlin. Now that I am to leave Ottawa I am beginning to know that I am fond of it and to know how much I shall miss my friends. The truth is that, much as I grumble about life in Ottawa, I have become attached to the place. Today I took my farewell walk along the terrace behind the Houses of Parliament and looked down on that scene that I know so well — the noble wide-flowing river, the Laurentian hills changing colour with every shift of light, and the silvery spires of the Basilica in the middle distance. Then I came back through the quiet tree-lined streets of Centretown, past the sensible red-brick mid-Victorian residences, the ponderous palaces of the lumber barons, and here and there a turreted fantasy, porch and balcony adorned with tortured woodwork. Our own apartment is in the upper floors of this old house, the bedrooms high among the top branches of the trees. In summer the sunlight on the shabby carpets is mottled in a changing leaf pattern; there are sun patches as warm as a summer beach and cooler spots where the leaves keep out the sun. This has become our home, more so than any Embassy could be. Our friends are here—we have become part of this closely knit community. Mike Pearson says that he saw very little sign of my new sentimentality about Ottawa until the day of my appointment abroad.

Bonn

When I took up my post as Ambassador to Bonn, the occupation of Germany by the Allied Powers was not yet ended, although official relations with the German government were becoming increasingly close. It was difficult not to think of the Germans with suspicion as the dangerous ex-enemy. The psychological and human breach had not had time to heal — much deeper ran the horror excited by the obscenities of the concentration camps and the brutish nastiness of the Nazi régime which stained the German name. The Germans, for their part, treated the representatives of the victors with the respect which Authority has always commanded in them. There was no resistance and no servility, but the acceptance of a fact — the fact of defeat. While one's social dealings with the Germans were friendly enough, there was too much on both sides that could not be spoken of, or forgotten, to make for real ease. During my years in Bonn this situation was changing. The German people were finding renewed confidence in themselves, the "economic miracle" of recovery was on the way. Germany under Adenauer's guidance was showing itself in advance of France and Britain in understanding the future role of Europe and was becoming the favoured friend of the United States. As the war receded and the Cold War intensified, we increasingly shared fears and interests with the Germans, who were soon to become allies. Then, too, with the ending of the Occupation there came an abrupt change in the attitude of the population. The measured deference due the former

Occupying Powers disappeared with almost startling rapidity. At the same time a most definite note of equality — sometimes of superiority — came into German voices. The socially false situation of the Occupation period was over — it was possible to have German friends. I think some of these changes may be found reflected in the small mirror of the diaries.

May 15, 1954 — Bonn

It is a glorious May morning. We are just off to Assmannshausen on the Rhine for the weekend. The Cadillac, with friendly and respectful chauffeur (ex-German Army), will draw up in front of the door at precisely 11 a.m. Our luggage will be carried from the door to the car by the amiable Erich, the butler, who will bow us off the premises. The excellent Lena, the lady's-maid, is now engaged in pressing Sylvia's underclothes in the linen room. The parlour-maid has just brought me on a silver salver my Ottawa dentist's bill, which I am afraid to open. The major-domo, Rudolf (ex-Rommel's army), has just presented to me the new gardener, an ex-sergeant-major in the Wehrmacht. So this is the way the War ends! No one could stay sulky on such a fine day with so many people devoting themselves with such cheerfulness to meeting one's every wish. No wonder our heads of mission get an inflated idea of themselves.

May 17, 1954

Just back from our visit to Assmannshausen. A sunny, happy little interlude. Dinner on the terrace looking across the Rhine under arches of wisteria to the accompaniment of sentimental music, drinking lots of red champagne which doesn't make you drunk but gives you the illusion that you can waltz. We did some rough-and-ready waltzing at a small nearby café. Sitting at the table on the terrace by the Rhine I was overcome by a sentimental mood, no doubt inspired by the red champagne but also by the Rhineland atmosphere. The pleasure of intimate talk about feelings, about life, a kind of nostalgia for romantic happiness (for you are looking into the eyes of the other one) — it is the return of the mood of youth, of youth that talks more than it does and dreams more than either, a mood which in New York would seem inconceivably dated, in Paris — beside the point. In Germany I find myself often thinking of the French, their cutting edge of style, the finality of their speech, their contemptuous impatience of blunders. As for Germany, if it is not like England it is not like anything, and of course it is not like England; yet every now and then at the corner of one of those suburban streets, or in the face of a schoolboy, or in the unexpected identity of a word in the language, there is a resemblance, the more disconcerting because the Germans seem so profoundly alien. As for me, I like my foreigners foreign. "Vive la France!"

June 2, 1954

This house in the Linden Allee, Cologne, which is the Embassy residence was built by the owner of a chain of stores in the characterless red-brick suburban style of the 1920s, so different from the ambitious, uninhibited monstrosities of pre-1914 German capitalist mansions. Almost the whole of this bourgeois residential part of Cologne escaped the bombing which wrecked the old medieval city and demolished the factories and the workers' quarters.

There is a garden full of rambler roses on trellises. There is breakfast on the pillared terrace. There are drinks in the evening, when the weather allows, sitting on garden chairs watching the birds poking about in the bowl of the fountain, where a single jet of water gently pisses. There is, of course, a swimming-pool and, next to the pool, a barbecue, the creation of my predecessor as ambassador — a shrewd, kind Western Canadian judge with a folksy vein to which we also owe the tooth-mugs in the bathroom with their alarming inscription "O wad some Power the giftie gie us / To see oursels as ithers see us".

Inside the house the rooms are well-spaced and tall. There is a vista from the marble-paved hall of flowers against the tapestry. There is a colossal fireplace. There is a candelabra hanging from the ceiling composed of bronze cupids which some previous occupant thought fit to clothe with little gilt jock-straps. On the terrace, imprisoned in a wooden packing-case, is a vast male marble nude which used to be in the hall. My predecessors could not live with him. Some day I plan an unveiling ceremony. Supplies and Properties of the Department of External Affairs have repainted formerly dark walls and ceilings of the interior of the house in an effort to induce cheerfulness. All the furniture has been re-covered in bright materials, with a fondness — almost amounting to a mania — for brilliant, strident yellow. Upstairs, *tout le confort moderne* — yet I think the big marble bathrooms stink like badgers' dens. Something wrong with the elaborate German plumbing. The house is pleasant enough to live in, but I hate the German servants' practice of locking the doors and windows from the inside at night. Down come steel shutters over all the ground-floor windows while the butler locks the doors from within and retires with the keys. I have now stopped him from doing this. It gives me the feeling of being incarcerated in a private lunatic asylum.

June 8, 1954

Developing an anonymous public face which expresses only cautious benevolence, controlling the spasms of nervous exasperation or high spirits, getting into the groove, the ambassadorial groove. It is a game, like learning German. Whether it is a game worthy of a grown man I cannot say.

How fortunate it is that the Embassy residence is in Cologne rather than Bonn. For Bonn, like most arbitrarily designated political capitals without a metropolitan tradition, is hard to love. The Germans themselves certainly do not love it. No doubt once as a university town it had its charm, before the politicians and the bureaucracy moved in and the new styleless government office buildings sprouted. In its environs are neat, agreeable residences suitable for residence by civil servants. Its admirers say that "it is a good place to bring up children" — an unenticing recommendation to childless adults like Sylvia and myself. Also in Bonn is the enclave (known locally as the Gold Coast) where the large American community of diplomats and officials is concentrated. There it is possible to purchase at the PX stores all sorts of American goods and to dispense with German shops. There, too, is the American Club, to which we Canadians have kindly been given courtesy membership and where cocktails are properly mixed and Germany seems further away than the Burning Tree Golf Club, Washington, D.C. In Zittelmannstrasse is the Canadian Chancery, to which I am conveyed every weekday in the official car via the Cologne-Bonn autobahn. The Chancery is modestly housed in a medium-sized villa. Its outlook is pleasantly pastoral. At the end of the quiet street is a rough, grassy field where sheep browse — a reminder that until recently this was a village lane on the outskirts of the town. Beyond the field the land slopes down through a municipal park of repellent aspect to the Rhine — an easy stroll to the river's bank when things in the office become too tedious. Bonn seems to me like an acquaintance — agreeable enough unless one does not fancy that particular mix: bureaucracy plus suburbia. Cologne is a very different matter. A flourishing centre of civilization for centuries and now what? The bombardment of Cologne during the war was concentrated on the ancient core of the city. In a series of hammer-blows the medieval walled town and most of its renowned monuments were reduced to rubble. The vast and overpraised cathedral and, oddly enough, the main railway station survived, with the tottering remains of some Romanesque churches and a medieval gateway opening on to the desolation within. Ten years after, on damp days, there hangs in the air of Cologne the stale stink of buried rubble and scorched beams that brings back to me London after a blitz. But here the destruction was more nearly total. When a city has been murdered, does its spirit survive the corruption of the body? The people of Cologne have kept their pride in their tradition of guild and church. Its affinities are with Trier and Aachen; the roots are Roman, the flowering was medieval. The corporate pride is exclusive — one hears its echo in the patronizing tone in which a citizen of Cologne speaks of upstart Düsseldorf, alien Berlin, or Americanized Frankfurt. I have no part in all this — I am an outsider to these memories and to the daily life of the city. Yet I feel an absurd borrowed sense of superiority when I say, "*We* live in Cologne," as though it were grander to inhabit a noble ruined city than neat, middle-class Bonn.

June 12, 1954

Back from Berlin today, from a visit to the Canadian Military Mission there which comes under my authority. The Berliners are stout-hearted, with a front-line mentality, like Londoners during the war. They are condescending about Bonn, which they despise as provincial and as being remote from daily contact with the enemy (now the Russians). Visited the reception centre where the refugees from East Germany are given physical examinations and kept overnight before being sent to the refugee camps. The medical side of it is under Frau Doktor Gerhard, a tough sergeant-major of a woman of seventy, full of humour and magnetism. She has seventeen doctors working under her.

What struck one was the smoothness of the organization, the incredible cleanness, the neatness of all the buildings in which thousands of refugees are housed. Not a scrap of paper lying on the floors, all clothes neatly folded in the dormitories. This mass of humanity, mostly rather dirty poor people with their miscellaneous belongings, passes through these buildings, living there without squalor or confusion. Imagine what it would be in France! More surprising was the humanity which seemed to accompany this efficiency, especially in the children's quarters, where little blue-eyed, flaxen-haired children of four and five were sitting round tables in pretty, airy nurseries playing with blocks with nurses who seemed kind and devoted. Even the quarters of the criminals and prostitutes who had slipped over the line to the transit camp were spotlessly clean. Did those who made the concentration camps make this?

I went to the interrogation of a woman member of the East German police who said she had deserted to come to the West, but who was suspected of being an East German spy. Narrow face, thin-lipped mouth, blank blue eyes. Something cold-blooded and vapid about her. She recited her story in a high, unfaltering voice, like a learned lesson. As a liar she failed by being too word-perfect. Age about twenty-two, formerly a saleswoman in a small town, then a private, later an officer, in the East German secret police, denounced a woman friend of hers to the police and was herself denounced to the police by her father because she had a boyfriend in West Berlin, hence her flight. She struck me as the type from which the Nazi women jailers came. As a saleswoman no doubt she was efficient, but would have been just as efficient at work in a gas chamber, and would have enjoyed the latter more.

Spent the day walking the streets of Berlin. Among the ruins are the new buildings. Some of the monumental buildings of the past survive like great mastodons of a vanished epoch. In a pile of rubble there would be an ornate doorway decorated with mouldering caryatids and leading to nothing.

June 14, 1954

"'Damn' braces, 'bless' relaxes." Got up in a bad temper and found this quite useful stiffening during the day. Herr Kleiber, Chef de Cabinet of the President of the Republic, called and was very critical of the French. It is impossible to defend the French behaviour over the European Defence Community, but none the less it is irritating to have to listen to the Germans sitting in judgement on them, and galling to sense — under their "more in sorrow than in anger" attitude — their contempt for French pretensions, their self-satisfaction with their own record. I am afraid that "rather a Frenchman wrong than a German right" is hardly a possible answer.

Received by Chancellor Adenauer. The more I see of him the more impressed I am by him. He is a very wise and a very wily old man, much subtler than the other German politicians, making them seem raw and provincial.

June 17, 1954

Unity Day celebration at the Bundeshaus* of the 17th June risings in Berlin against the Soviet occupants. Looking down from the diplomatic gallery at the rows of middle-aged, middle-class deputies, all listening with restrained boredom to long-winded speeches, I thought, "And these are the chaps who used to listen to Hitler."

The ugliness of the Cologne population is something to be marvelled at. In the crowd outside Cologne Cathedral today listening to the Corpus Christi celebrations, there was not one attractive woman; unglossy, dry hair, pasty or weather-beaten complexions, little boot-button

*German parliament.

eyes, sack-like clothes, dun-coloured or grey, big bottoms, and a stumping, hausfrau walk. And so many of the men with long, badly modelled noses and high cheek-bones, with something goose-like about their movements.

Last night, dinner at the French Ambassador's (François-Poncet's) château on the top of a hill overlooking the Rhine. The choice of the house was designed to impress the Germans and everybody else with the presence of a Great Power — France. It is more successful in general effect than on closer scrutiny. An "eighteenth-century" French château, in fact built by a rich German industrialist in 1912. There were the much-talked-of footmen in scarlet satin knee-breeches and there was the much-heralded cuisine. Not a single German there, all diplomats and their wives, several pretty Latin American women, bored with Bonn and living for their next shopping expedition to Paris. Agreeably frivolous conversation of the kind that the presence of Germans makes difficult. A little diplomatic world under a glass dome.

June 23, 1954

I am trying to learn German. The woman who is teaching me is making me learn the German version of Little Red Riding Hood by heart. This is the only German I so far know. Last night we went to a German dinner party. I was seated between two wives of German high officials, stout bodies, little gold crosses on chains round their necks, reddish faces, not a word of English. Finally, unable to stand the silence any longer, I turned from one to the other and launched into Red Riding Hood. "Red Riding Hood comes into the wood. She is not frightened of the wolf. When she sees the grandmother she asks, 'Why have you got such big eyes? Why have you got such big ears?'" All this in quite fluent German. The two ladies stared at me in dumb amazement. One of them asked on a questioning note, "Bitte, Exzellenz?" Otherwise, no reaction. However, the German official on the other side of the table, who could not hear what I was saying, came up to me afterwards and complimented me on my fluent German.

July 18, 1954

The servants in this house impose their own restrictions. Sylvia and I must sit solemnly at the long dinner table, taste the wine, be waited upon by butler and maid. When I leave the house for the office I must be bowed to the courtyard gate by the butler, who hands over the red leather dispatch box to the waiting chauffeur. It is impossible to create confusion in this house. Throw your clothes on the floor at night, they are picked up and sorted out by morning. How is one to resist this smoothing-out, flattening-out process which makes an ambassador of you from the collar-button inward?

July 26, 1954

Where are all the former Nazis in Germany? I mean, physically, where are they? They are certainly not to be met in Bonn, or, if they are, they are well disguised. On the evidence of one's eyes and ears one would be led to believe that the entire German population was subjugated by Hitler and a small gang of his criminal associates. Another curious thing is that of the many ex-officers of the German army I have met, none mention serving on the Western Front. With Rommel in Africa — yes, but mostly they talk of their service on the Eastern Front against the Russians, and the theme of their story is that *they* recognized the communist menace, that *they* were fighting to defend Western civilization against a danger which we were too blind to recognize. As to their casualties in Russia, they are mentioned in a tone which suggests "these died not only for us but for you." If the Nazis have gone to ground, the Jews have vanished into the gas ovens. I have only met one Jew since I have been here. When the word "Jew" is mentioned among the Germans, a self-conscious silence sets in, as if a social gaffe had been made.

The Germans in their dealings with us seem on their best behaviour. Cautious, patient, kindly, friendly people without a trace of arrogance. It is as though they had all received a mysterious order from a hidden leader as to how they should behave.

These new bifocals are tormenting me. I feel like a horse wearing a bit for the first time, or as a boy when I had to wear woolly underwear. And to think that I have to live with these for the rest of my life!

October 10, 1954

A Sunday of getting into the car and motoring somewhere for lunch together and afterwards seeing old churches and castles. The abbey of Maria Lach has stood there by its lake for a thousand years, or as near as makes no difference. It is big, all right, but is it beautiful? At any rate it is startling, like meeting an elephant in a glade. Lunch in a manor-house-turned-motel, the family portraits looking down on fat men and women eating. Then to an ancient church near Bonn. The church made me shiver, and coming back in the car I felt a sudden, shuddering, Sunday-afternoon melancholy. In the mist, youths in belted mackintoshes down to their ankles, and old women in black suits, were stumping along. I wanted to get right into bed and start making love, as a sign of life in the face of those mineral monuments and vegetable people.

November 25, 1954

Dined again with the François-Poncets, guests consisting of rich Rhineland industrialists and their wives. They came from Duisburg and Düsseldorf with their diamonds and minks. The atmosphere was so thick with money that one felt it could be a subject embarrassing in any connection to mention. These people seemed to be a world in itself of big money, very different and quite apart from the local nobility and gentry. The shabby-grand Wittgensteins and their friends live in the lodges of their castles with halls decorated with antlers and no springs in the drawing-room sofa. They are the easiest to get along with. They almost all had English governesses and talk a fluent English interspersed with pre-War slang and Mayfair expressions of the 1930s. They had no opportunity to catch up during the War. All talk of the Nazis with a sort of snobbish disgust. All the men seemed to have served in the army on the Eastern Front.

November 26, 1954

Lunch today with Brentano, who is to be the next Foreign Minister. I had heard that he was a stupid man, but I do not think so. Yet he seemed hardly tiresome enough to make a successful politician. He confirmed what I hear from everywhere, that there is no enthusiasm in this country for rearmament; no one seems keen about it in industry, in labour, or among the intelligentsia. We lunched in icy draughts at the Redoute Club and drank brandy after lunch, which made me sleepy, so that when I left Brentano at the door I absent-mindedly said "Good-night" to him at two-thirty in the afternoon.

The other night François-Poncet was talking about *Le Grand Meaulnes*. He says it is German and not French in its kind of romantic inspiration. Curious, I have often thought of that book since coming to this country.

The Rhineland has a nervous, boring, neurotic atmosphere but is not commonplace. The obsessive feeling of the place persists, putting everything slightly out of true, distorting, casting strange lights and shadows, always with a persistent, sinister undertone. It is hard to render in words — in music?

Of the social situation and our relations with the Germans, Elizabeth Bowen says, "It is a great, bright, ghastly smile covering an incurably false position." Elizabeth's new book, *A World of Love*, is marvellous, a masterpiece of her own genius. She wrote a lot of it in the sitting-room of this house when she was staying here, and on the verandah of that small hotel in Bonn.

December 20, 1954 — Hotel Plaza-Athénée, Paris

I am here for Mike Pearson's* visit, spending my time with the Canadian Delegation. Rye whisky in the hotel sitting-room, then a straggle of the delegation, a couple of secretaries, and a tame journalist; we all drift out to some unlikely restaurant or night-club for the evening. All day is spent wandering round hotel corridors, waiting for the Minister to come in or to go out, waiting for the typing to be finished, knocking at doors with Draft 3 of the speech in one's hand. Where *is* the Minister? Out buying a present for his wife? A good dose of Canadians. When I went to the plane to see them off I felt I'd like to stay and arrive home for Christmas, coming down in the snow and icy wind at Dorval, flying on down to Halifax. I thought what hell it would be to be an exile, to see a plane leaving for Canada and to know that I could never go back.

December 24, 1954 — Cologne

Wild wind blowing. Yesterday it blew the scaffolding off Cologne Cathedral. It came hurtling down from the high tower into a narrow street, scattering the people like a thunderbolt from Heaven and sending them scurrying into side-streets and shop fronts for shelter. The household is disorganized by the new dachshund puppy we have just

*Pearson was then Secretary of State for External Affairs.

bought. A long-haired dachshund, an attractive little creature. It peed in the middle of the new dining-room carpet where no table, chair, or rug can conceal the damage.

The Vice-Chancellor, Blücher, came to lunch. He has just returned from representing Germany at the Queen's coronation in London. His eyes filled with tears when he spoke of the significance and beauty of the coronation ceremony and of the kindness of Princess Alice. He said that here was a lesson for Germany, and expressed deep nostalgia for the monarchy. Blücher struck me as rather commonplace and absurdly vain. When we were talking of different German accents and which was the best, he said, "I do not want to boast, but you could not possibly do better than listen to my accent." He is anxious to play a part in foreign affairs and he indicates that his views are wider and less narrowly political than those of Adenauer.

December 26, 1954

Overcast weather, rushing wind, mire in the fields, swollen, dirty little rivers, trees snapped by the gale. We are sitting in the upstairs sitting-room among the presents for today's children's Christmas party—children of the staff, Canadian and German. The presents include Indian headdresses, teddy bears, jigsaw puzzles. The radio is going full blast but I am afraid to touch it for fear of breaking it for the third time. The puppy, now called Popski, is locked in the bathroom and barking incessantly. The German servants are delighted with their presents, delighted with our Christmas party, the cook making endless cakes covered with marzipan flowers.

January 1, 1955

Had an obscene-looking upside-down egg with shreds of ham adhering to it for breakfast. Began rereading

Swann's Way in my bath and thought of when I first read it in a cold bath in my lodgings in Earl's Court Road over the creamery during the heat wave of 1932 when I was earning four pounds a week as a reporter for the *Evening Standard*, and then later in Paris she and I read Proust aloud to each other in the intervals of making love.

January 2, 1955

A New Year's party last night, all English. A lady called Mrs. Tusket said, "Hamlet was only fourteen years of age." How does she know? Did some friend of his tell her? She said that it is a part that is played too old by men too old for it. Sat next to an Englishman after dinner who said, "After nine years in Germany I have been offered a job in Rhodesia, so my wife and I are off. Quite remunerative, the job, with a house thrown in." I asked, "Is Rhodesia a colony on its own or part of a federation?" "No idea," he said, "never been in Africa except in Tangiers for one day and that's no guide."

January 3, 1955

Holiday. Spent the day playing with the dog, reading *Swann's Way*. Tea before the fire, house still hung with Christmas cards, greyness outside. Hamlet was not fourteen as Mrs. Tusket pretends, but over twenty-four, as the Anglican archdeacon has proved to me from the evidence of the Yorick scene.

The evening party last night — danced with a pretty Irish woman. Asked her, "What do women mean by security?" She said, "I could give you a ribald answer to that one. We want to know *it*'s there. Anyway," she said, glancing out of the corner of her green eyes, "that's one thing I've never bothered my head about. Security I care nothing for."

January 9, 1955

The servants are calling for Popski up and down the house. They adore him and spoil him incessantly. He will be lucky if he doesn't turn into a self-centred little neurotic.

The German men are good company. They enjoy jokes, although preferring the one about the other man slipping on the banana peel. They have a streak of adolescent cynicism. But they are not hypocrites, they are not platitudinous. Although they may be deceitful about their intentions, they are frank and rather indiscreet about their feelings. They are by nature terrific talkers. Their most striking lack seems to be grace, style, elegance. The so-called festival gaiety of the Rhineland depends on immense quantities of beer or wine, and ends in moon-faced boorishness.

A bold, unstable race. They have the attraction of vitality and the fascination which the adventurous exercise. They are not a middle-aged race as so many of the English and French are (not to mention Canadians).

I was thinking today about the ups and downs through which so many of the diplomats here in Bonn have passed during the course of the war years. So many of the Europeans have been in exile from their own countries, the Dutch Ambassador for one, living in a bed-sitting-room in London, then — with the liberation of the Netherlands — becoming Governor General of Indonesia in a palace with a hundred servants. François-Poncet, *Figaro* hack, French Ambassador, a prisoner of the Gestapo, and now Ambassador again. As for the Asians, many of them have served their term in prisons during the colonial period, whereas the communist diplomats have of course had a training as revolutionaries. Yet all this variety of experience is triumphed over by the extraordinary force of the convention of the diplomatic corps, a caste which envelops everyone, so tenacious of its privileges that it has maintained a sort of eighteenth-century enclave in the modern world, ruled by privilege — manners good, bad, and indifferent — and, above all, rank.

A Bavarian gentleman came to lunch today. Brilliantly blue eyes a little too expressive, a bachelor, takes immense trouble over his fingernails. He had an odd expression for near-Nazis, saying they had "a brownish tinge" (an allusion to the Brown Shirts). He said, "I never had any sympathy for the Nazis, yet after all even I fought in Hitler's army. But then, you people were allied with communism. So there you are. I remember the first time I said 'Heil Hitler'. It was to get into a military hospital to take a present to a sick friend; otherwise they would not have let me in. But I was never a Nazi. Not that I suppose you will want to check up on that, but it is a fact." I felt like saying, "It's not your guilt or lack of guilt that interests me, it's your experiences. Tell me what it was like to live through all that."

There was a domestic crisis today. The butler, Erich, has been having an affair with one of the housemaids. His wife has found out and insists that he should leave and go to Munich to start a restaurant with her. In talking to me he burst into tears, saying he didn't want to leave and that women were terrible — the same all the world over — so unreasonable. In fact I am very anxious to keep Erich as he is an extremely good butler with a sympathetic although weak character. I have suggested to him that I would pay the rent of his wife's house in Munich if she wanted to go there and he could join her at some indefinite period in the future. He seems inclined to accept this, but no doubt when his wife has talked to him he will change his mind.

January 12, 1955

Started the day with a very irritating conversation with François-Poncet on the telephone in which he got the better of me. What a genius the French have for putting one in the wrong. It is a great mistake to discuss business with them in their own language. Even a stupid French-man, which François-Poncet certainly is not, can score off one with that weapon in hand.

A professor of chemistry from Bonn University to lunch today. He talked about conditions in his former university of Leipzig. He is in touch with his colleagues there and says that the régime bears hardest on law and the humanities. Scientists have no trouble and are doing very good work, with excellent pay.

January 13, 1955

I cut my throat this morning when shaving and have gone about all day looking like a failed suicide. The sitting-room is full of hyacinths, white, pink, and mauve, and smells delicious. I must go and dress for the fancy-dress ball at the French Embassy. False beard. Erich says it makes me look like a Russian prince. I think it makes me look like a commissar. Sylvia looks lovely in her costume.

January 15, 1955

I am certainly lucky in the staff of the Embassy. John Starnes, the Counsellor, would make a better Ambassador than I. He has an acute, questioning mind and a grasp of German affairs. He is also a companion and friend with whom one never has a dull moment. Helen, his wife, is a delight — lovely to look at, funny, and equal to any occasion. Pam McDougall, the First Secretary, is handsome, humorous, and exceptionally able. The Air Attaché, Doug Edwards, and his wife Lois have become what one could call "boon companions" of ours. We knew them in Paris days when he was at the Embassy there. He is the easiest of company and she is witty and attractive. The younger members of the staff, Peyton Lyon and Frank Stone, are among the most promising of their generation in the public service.

January 16, 1955

Luncheon party here today, including the Wittgensteins and her mother, old Countess Metternich. She was English by birth, the daughter of an admiral, and her mother was a Miss Kenny from Halifax, Nova Scotia. She said to me in earnest tones, "Have you ever seen Thornvale, outside Halifax? It must be a beautiful house. My mother always told me that it was far finer than the Metternich castle." In fact, Thornvale is a Victorian wooden villa. I was much amused by this piece of Nova Scotian loyalty and I backed it up strongly, saying, "Your mother was quite right. Thornvale is indeed magnificent and makes most German castles seem quite insignificant." Countess Metternich gave a sigh of deep satisfaction. The Wittgensteins are becoming friends. She is very pretty and a great charmer — she certainly charms me.

Little Prince Wittgenstein embarked on a series of questions about Canada. "Canada is part of the Commonwealth but not a province of the United Kingdom?" I agreed. "Why then do you have a Governor General?" I tried to sketch out the constitutional position of the Commonwealth and the monarchy. He looked very suspicious, as though I was concealing something, probably our subordination to Britain.

January 21, 1955

Went to an English cocktail party in honour of the new clergyman just out from England. The English colony is riddled with fights over running the English church here.

A member of the German Socialist Party (SPD) to lunch. A clever, cynical little man, but sincere in his immovable suspicion of creating a German army in any form. He kept on saying, "We do not know what it will be like. We can only judge by the record." Indeed, if we encourage the Germans to be rearmed it will be very largely our responsibility. There is no enthusiasm for it, partly due to full employment in this country, partly to the fact that the Germans have felt protected by the Occupation forces and now by NATO troops. The mood of the younger generation seems to be one of indifference to slogans and causes. They had enough of that growing up under the Nazis. They want to settle down, get good jobs. There are many early marriages. I was talking the other day to one of the refugees from the lost territories in Prussia, where he had been a landlord. He said he and his generation would never be reconciled to the loss of these lands, nor would this generation of German refugees from Czechoslovakia ever accept their exile, but he said his own sons were typical of the new generation in being bored with the whole subject and wanting to settle down to a good paying job in Düsseldorf or Frankfurt.

On the other hand, many people with whom I have talked believe that once the new German army is in existence the Germans will toe the line, and that the German tradition of militarism is deeper than any passing mood. One of the NATO military attachés said to me the other day, "Good martial music and a few parades and they will be back where they started." But the question is — do we want them back where they started? We can't have it both ways.

I had a long talk with Beaudissen the other day about all this. He is a German officer with an anti-Nazi record who is consultant to the German government on measures to be taken to ensure that the new German army will be different from the old, without its dangerous aggressive tendencies. He is a nice, well-meaning man but does not carry much conviction, at least to me. He talks of a citizen army, an army which would not feel itself separate from the people — not a state within a state, but an army of individuals who are not military robots but have a sense of belonging to the civilian community. He talked of a tank crew as the ideal size of the group where political discussion could develop individual initiative, and he linked this with the concept of mobility and the tendency away from the mass concentration of troops. He said that it was necessary to curb the caste character of the German army and make it more socially democratic. But he went on to admit that a great deal had been done in this way by Hitler, and that Hitler's army had been much more democratic in spirit and composition than any German army of the past. This social democratization had gone furthest in the air force, yet the air force was the most fanatically Nazi element in the armed forces. I imagine that this talk of democratizing the German army may be beating a dead horse and that the dangers in the future will not be from the remains of an hereditary officer corps but from those trained in the new tradition of German militarism — the ex-officers and NCOs of Hitler's army.

January 23, 1955

How I loathe dances. Why do I always drink too much at them? Why do I build up these killing hangovers? I should like to be living alone, or almost alone, by the sea somewhere, allowed three visitors a week, chosen by me, lots of books (and perfect eyesight to read indefinitely), solitary walks, and short sprees to places of my choice with people of my choice.

The Rhine is in flood up to the tops of the lamp-posts on the Rhine road outside the Bundestag. I was thinking this morning of my old boarding-school in Canada, a red-brick building on a hill, now — thank God — burnt down. There was one boy, a wall-eyed, bandy-legged, log-witted giant who hated me (or did I imagine that?) — at any rate, tormented me. I swore that later in life I should be revenged on this sadistic son-of-a-bitch. To my undying shame, when I met him in London in 1939 as a grown-up Toronto broker I not only did not kill him on sight, I shook hands with him, a betrayal of myself as a boy.

At that school the headmaster and most of the masters were Englishmen. The system of prefects, fagging, etc., was not natural to the Canadian scene any more than the cult of cricket. It was an alien system and I think it set up strains of which the boys were not conscious but which disturbed them. By 1922 or 1923 we had certainly ceased to be colonials but were not yet fully a nation. It was an Awkward Age. The idea of Empire, of which Canada was proud to be a part, was still alive to the older generation who sent their boys to this school, but my contemporaries were young Canadian nationalists without knowing it. Their Toronto conservative fathers imposed things English on them but they remained like a Sunday suit and stiff collar worn for the occasion. Nothing could stop the natural slip into North American habits. Old Silver Balls, as we called the headmaster, said he wanted the school to be "an oasis of monastic seclusion in the desert of commercial modernity". He got a horse-laugh from the boys. He was a Wykehamist and he wanted to make Wykehamists of these future Canadian brokers, bank managers, lawyers, and insurance men. His defeat was total. Although I had just come from an English school, I was a schoolboy and so, as a matter of course, on the other side of the barriers from the masters. Besides, I was not a natural Wykehamist.

The scene from my window this evening: Claus, the cook, is standing at the door in his white chef's cap, which he never removes indoors or out, except I suppose when he goes to bed. The door has been thrown open by the butler to let Popski out for a pee in the garden. The night-watchman is standing by with a torch to light Popski's way and the chauffeur is watching the gate lest he should slip out on to the road.

Lunch today with Charles and Natasha Johnston of

the British Embassy. They are the people I like best here.
The new Greek Ambassador and his wife were there. She is
a big ox of a woman with dyed hair and a loud voice, a
wonderful mimic, very funny, just what we need to
lighten life in Bonn.

There is an article about me in *Time* magazine which
says, among other things, that I have been "pepping up
diplomatic dinner parties for twenty years". What a
ghastly epitaph for my tombstone!

January 29, 1955

Dinner with Terence Prittie and his wife. He is the
Manchester Guardian man, an Anglo-Irish Etonian, intelligent and entertaining. When he puts on his "granny"
glasses he looks dreary and respectable; when he takes
them off he looks a little pugilistic. He has no faith
whatever in the changed character of the Germans and says
that Beaudissen will get nowhere in changing the German
military and that one day there will be a show-down
between the Protestant Church in the eastern zone and the
Communists over the future of East German youth. Sat
next to an Englishwoman at dinner who said, "My only
problem is that my son should be my daughter and my
daughter should be my son."

In the afternoon went to a German film, *Canaris*, in
Bonn. There was an old news film showing Hitler's entry
into Vienna. At his appearance the German audience burst
into laughter, mocking and hating laughter. It was an
extraordinary performance.

Diplomatic dinner in the evening. A terrible row
over the placing of the guests. No fewer than three ambassadresses claimed that they had been wrongly placed at
table, and one threatened to leave.

Popski is gnawing one of Sylvia's evening slippers.
Every time we try to get it from him he shoves it under the
sofa and when our backs are turned hauls it out again.

March 1, 1955

Alone in the house. Sylvia has flown to Canada to see her mother before she dies, if there is time. I felt so sorry for her as alone she stepped on to the plane to leave.

March 11, 1955

My official visit to Hamburg. This visit is going better than I expected and I may even do some good for German-Canadian relations. Dinner last night at the Anglo-German Club. Businessmen and consuls, Englishmen who had spent twenty, thirty, forty years in Hamburg and spoke German with old familiarity. Germans who had been born in Liverpool or educated in Scotland and spoke English with homely local accents acquired in their boyhood. It gave me an idea of the character of Hamburg as a twin sister of Liverpool or Glasgow, tied with England in peace or war for decades or centuries. I like this community of shipowners and merchants. I have been on a tour of the newly built areas of Hamburg, which cover the square miles of the densely built city totally destroyed in the three-day air-raids.

They are constructing a new city of space, light, greater privacy, and less density of population per acre — a planner's dream.

March 12, 1955

After dinner drank brandy with the British Consul and he took me for a tour of the Reeperbahn. A most unvicious place with the atmosphere of a Hammersmith palais de danse. A nude woman emerges from a bubble bath and an attendant showers the soap off her bottom, all to slow music, then up go the lights, dance music, a collection of women in snuff-coloured dresses or sweaters and skirts waiting to be danced with, waitresses or tarts tittering and drinking beer. At every corner nude displays and then a solo dance by a lady in a lace gown who represented refinement. It all seemed clean fun suitable for children and grandmothers. Indeed, there seemed to be a lot of grandmothers around, stout elderly bodies in groups or with their husbands. There seems nothing between these shows and brothels.

March 13, 1955

I had lunch yesterday at Friedrichsrühe with the Bismarcks. The house is situated in a great forest of firs and was destroyed by a bomb during the War, which also killed the Swiss Consul and his wife, who were staying at the time with the Bismarcks. The new house is built on the foundation of the old. Their house party was standing about in the drawing-room, talking. Then the door burst open and Prince and Princess Bismarck bounced in as if released from a circus cannon, he with a pink face and a pink carnation in his buttonhole, she a Swede with the "international society" manner, opening her ever-so-blue eyes very wide at one as she talked. Age around fifty, quick in conversation, mischievous and mocking. She has her social twin sisters in London, Paris, and New York. Her husband is a member of the Bundestag but he is not, I think, taken very seriously.

March 17, 1955

The day began badly. Popski escaped from his room and came into mine at five in the morning and woke me up. I lost my temper with the poor little bugger and began yelling at him like a banshee, and threw boots at him. All day I felt sad, sensual, and sloppy. Sylvia arrives today from Canada with her aunts, Elsie and Beatrice, who are coming to stay. I have been getting the servants to put flowers in their bedrooms; Claus is cooking up a steak-and-kidney pie for their lunch.

The possibility of nuclear warfare looms over all hopes. It looks as though this unhappy generation will have to pay an enormous overdue bill for all the follies and sins of the human race, and by comparison every previous generation, whatever its fate, may have been lucky not to be born in the twentieth century.

March 20, 1955

It is lovely having Sylvia back again. I am enjoying this visit of the old girls. Aunt Elsie (now seventy-five) is, of course, my old friend and ally. How many nights at her apartment at the Roxborough in Ottawa we have sat up together talking about life, love, and politics, and drinking whisky. I love her for her warm, generous heart and for being so funny, but she has got terribly deaf, and there is something touching about her impatience with her own deafness. She has still kept her wish for happiness and still suffers from childish disappointments. She says she hates old people, that they are empty of everything, like old paper bags blowing about. Perhaps I shall hate the old too when I am old. Being sorry for them gives me a feeling of being younger than I am. Talking of age, Aunt Beatrice is now eighty-seven. She is, as usual, full of stories of Dundarave, the Irish estate where she passed her married life — also long anecdotes beginning "On one occasion when we were staying at Brown's Hotel . . .", which is a signal that she will go on for twenty minutes. All the same, I admire her spirit and her toughness. She is perfect with the German servants, who appreciate her "grand manner" and respond to her bossiness. In some ways she is a natural German herself.

I can't think why I am haunted by that bloody boarding-school. Looking back it seems to me that a miasma of sexual prurience, excitement, and fear hung over those boring days and dream-filled nights. Of course, I was an insufferable boy — but who isn't, at fourteen?

Tomorrow is supposed to be the first day of spring, but still snow on the ground. Sylvia and Aunt Elsie have just left for church (Aunt Beatrice disapproves of religion). Popski is barking despairingly in the garden where he has been left to amuse himself for an hour. An unmistakably Sunday feeling in the house today. Can even the nuclear bomb change Sunday?

The Wittgensteins and old Countess Metternich to dinner last night. Countess Metternich and Aunt Beatrice are made for each other. Monica Wittgenstein was mocking the social aspirations of the Cologne bourgeoisie in tones familiar all the world over wherever the hard-up gentry talk of the newly cash-conscious.

At dinner at the Starneses' was a German ex-officer, a handsome bob-sleigh champion, who figure-skates near here. He had been on the Eastern Front and said that when the Germans came into the Ukraine he went with them right into the villages on his motor-bike and that the Ukrainians threw so many flowers and so much food and butter to the German troops that he was lucky to have his tin hat on or he would have been brained. He said all the Ukrainians wanted was independence, or at least a show of it, and if the Germans had pulled a Grand Duke out of Paris and set up a Ukrainian state they could have settled any quantity of Germans there and have secured the agricultural produce of the Ukraine. He went on, "None of you on your side would have cared and we could have got away with it, but that little Austrian pup Hitler had to go and blow up the holy places at Kiev and turn the people against the Germans. Then he imported narrow-minded German schoolmasters and made them Gauleiters who oppressed the people and lived on champagne. When the War began I thought it was a crusade against communism, but after serving on the Eastern Front I soon discovered that it was not a crusade. I had two old White Russian aunts living in Berlin as émigrées, naturally violently anti-communist, but as the campaigns on the Eastern Front went on and the destruction of Russian cities began, they began to say that this was a wicked war against Holy Russia and to listen to Stalin's speeches on the radio."

April 2, 1955

The two old girls are having a social success here. We have taken them round to a lot of parties and they seem to be very much enjoying themselves. Aunt Beatrice got into a misunderstanding yesterday at a diplomatic party with the South African Ambassador. She said, "I do not approve of your government's policies in South Africa." The Ambassador, thinking he was up against a gentle, liberal-minded old lady, began a long-winded explanation of how devoted his government was to the best interests of the black population when Beatrice interrupted him to say, "I don't mean that at all. I think you should take a much stronger line with them. Shoot them down if they give you any trouble."

Went into Cologne with the aunts. I had to stagger round the jewellery shops with them, carrying a bag of asparagus, vermouth, and cheese, while they had every diamond in Cologne out to compare unfavourably with their own rings. I cannot think that Aunt Beatrice needs any more rings. Her old hands are already laden with four outsize cat's-eyes, one large diamond, and one mammoth dark opal, known in the family as "the frog".

May 15, 1955

Chip Bohlen has suggested my flying to Moscow with him for a visit, as he is American Ambassador there now. I think I might do this. I am in the mood for a fresh start. From now on not a single day is to be thrown away as you chuck in an unsatisfactory hand at poker. Today is windy, sunny, lilacs blowing in the wind, everything in bloom, a feeling of exhilaration like a morning in one's youth, a restless mood, up one minute, down the next. Yet one must be wary of the dreams and projects which swarm in one's mind as the sun plays on lilacs and chestnuts as you walk quickly past the neat white houses of the English suburb of Cologne to buy the Sunday papers.

June 12, 1955

Sitting alone on a bench in Sud-Park with my eyes closed, thinking that I used to imagine what it would be like to be an old man sitting alone on a bench in a park. Perhaps when my heart grows as small as a peanut I shall be a cheerful and sociable old man like my grandfather and like I was in my heartless youth. There is rain on the rhododendrons and the roses. A brooding resentment settles in this climate like a low cloud that hangs never far away over the Rhine Valley. Then brief passages of sunlit elation. Yesterday — or was it the day before? — the clergyman came to lunch. "Blessed be the poor in spirit," he quoted. What does that mean? I understood better today when Mrs. Chichester came to lunch, so smug in good works, so qualified for salvation. She was indeed "rich in spirit", quite overpoweringly so.

Now what could be fairer than this rose garden with the roses just out, a swimming-pool waiting for me around the corner, caviare for lunch with a little white wine, a valet tenderly brushing my morning coat. My hopes and unsung struggles would make the average man laugh himself sick and say, "Affectation and nonsense."

Reading André Maurois's account of George Sand's love life and her ghastly, claggy letters to her lovers. How did they put up with her? How much nicer to have had as a mistress an obedient, co-operative, brown-skinned maiden who could not speak a word of any known language but was graceful and usually half-nude, and to live with her in a clean, sunny house in a valley in Ceylon.

July 1, 1955

Our National Day. A reception here this afternoon —
five hundred guests and it will certainly rain. It started out
fine this morning but is already clouding over and the
birds by their twitterings are obviously expecting rain.
Diana Cooper and Frank and Kitty Giles* staying here.
Frank is so intelligent, so open to new ideas and impressions. As for Kitty, she makes everything and everyone
around her alive — who could not love her? Everything
went swimmingly. We sat out a lot on the terrace among
the roses while the atomic air exercise "Carte Blanche"
went roaring over the garden. Diana was adorable but has
the bad effect on me of making everyone else seem dull.

Sat next to the Ethiopian Minister's wife at dinner
last night and fell a little in love with her — an exquisite,
intelligent, dark statuette dressed by Dior.

There is not enough to do in the office and I hate an
office that is going at a slow pace where every little snippet
of business is magnified to fill in time. I have a goose of a
German student as a language teacher. He stinks so much
in this hot weather that I can hardly bear having him
sitting next to me on the sofa.

July 23, 1955

Haus-Assen. Staying with the Von Galens for the
week in their schloss in Westphalia. A family of five
daughters, a refugee aunt from the Sudetenland, an English school-friend of the daughters, the only son of the
house, an Oxford friend of his, an Austrian archduke, and
two little local barons are all staying in this moated
sixteenth-century house. (The moat is solid with a beautifully coloured green scum with a dead fish on the surface
and some very live ducks swimming about in it.) The Von

*Frank Giles, British journalist, since Editor of the *Sunday Times*, and
his wife, Lady Katherine Giles.

Galens very welcoming, extremely nice. Their girls with English-schoolgirl voices calling "Mummy" and "Daddy" from the garden. Racing Demon after dinner. My host explained to me the difference between the barbarous Prussians and the West Germans, whose civilization goes back to Charlemagne. There were so many at dinner that the young ones sat at what they called "the cat's table", the one for the children. I wished I had five daughters. We have a circular room in Biedermeier style with a balcony over the moat.

We all walked over to the vegetable garden and ate currants and raspberries, talked in a desultory way, drifted down lanes and around farm buildings. Their son is on vacation from Oxford — Christchurch — a breath of under-graduate goings-on.

July 25, 1955

A long argument last night after dinner with Mike Handler of the *New York Times*, who attributes all the evil in the world to Adenauer and Dulles and says that as Adenauer is now in fact United States Secretary of State, why not name him so? An American woman was there, rather drunk. She says that all her friends in New York came from the three per cent of successful people in *all* fields.

Sylvia says that this is the end of summer. The heat is over. The roses in the garden are dead or dying. The pink ramblers look rather disgusting in their vegetable decay. There is a feeling of break-up in the house. We had last night one of our last and least successful dinner parties of the season. The butler, Erich, is leaving. The other ser-vants are anxious to go on their holidays and so am I. We can hardly be bothered to train the dog any more. We shan't be seeing him again for a month and then perhaps we shall all be different, including Popski. Our first year

in Germany is over. I want to get away now from this
queasy climate, the quilt of low cloud, hazy in heat, dark
in dank weather.

August 7, 1955

A newly appointed special consultant in the German
Foreign Office came to dinner last night. He has spent the
greater part of his life in Russia, as has his wife. Their
parents were members of the German colony in St.
Petersburg. They have the accent and the charm and the
naturalness of manner of White Russians but are very
German. They were complaining that the Russians in
their own view know everything better than everyone else,
but I felt inclined to reply, "So do the Germans, so do the
French, all three are know-it-all nations. The English do
not know it all and don't wish to. They just know that they
are better."

January 26, 1956

I am getting quite fond of the new butler, Karl, but
my God he is obstinate! This morning I asked him to pack
my dark-blue suit to go to Soest. He said, "The suit is dark
but it is not blue," to which I replied, "Please pack my
dark-blue suit." We stared at each other without yielding.

Motored to Soest in wind and snow. Great double
trucks interlocked in collision along the autobahn.
Volkswagens crushed like tin cans. The Germans are the
most frantic drivers in the world and their roads are strewn
battlegrounds. Got to Soest five minutes before dinner,
changed in a rush with my drink in my hand. Roger
Rowley is in command of the Canadian Brigade. This was
the occasion of the visit of General Gale, the Commander-
in-Chief of the British Army on the Rhine, and Lady Gale,
who had come over for the night in their private diesel
train from their schloss, which Lady Gale tells me has four

drawing-rooms and takes twenty-one servants to run. General "Windy" Gale is like a bloodshot old bulldog barking amiably. His hackles rose a bit at the sight of an Ambassador, and a Canadian Ambassador at that. I dare say he thinks it quite superfluous for us to have any diplomatic representation at all, but we circled around each other in fine fettle. Lady Gale was the success of the party—red hair, plump, fiftyish, shrewd, and good fun. Played games until three in the morning. The Army are tough. Roger came into my room at dawn while I was asleep—in uniform, off to manoeuvres.

January 27, 1956

I lunched today with Von Welk, who looks after Canadian affairs in the German Foreign Office. We meet for lunch twice a month at the Adler, a restaurant that specializes in the food the Germans best understand— venison. Von Welk and I discuss our problems in Canadian-German relations. He snorts and crinkles up his brown eyes, looking at me with a dachshund expression. For some reason I am much drawn to this unattractive man with whom I seem to have nothing in common. He is stiff and rude at times, but never pompous. He can be malicious, but he is not boring. There is something dowdy about him which inspires a sort of confidence. He might do a double-cross, but he himself is not a lie.

February 4, 1956

Have been staying with Norman and Jetty Robertson in London, where he is now High Commissioner. Norman was at his most delightful, with his wonderful, wide-ranging curiosity and interest in everything and everybody, his pleasure in his own cleverness, his mixture of boldness in thought and of caution. Isn't he in the long run profoundly on the side of constituted authority although he enjoys dissecting it? He is a non-believer of Presbyterian origin. How different in mentality is a Presbyterian from an Anglican agnostic, not to mention a Roman Catholic one. You can renounce your own faith but its particular imprint remains. I measure myself against Norman and I know that he is a wiser and better man than I am. I came away even fonder of him than I was before and I tremble to think what he would make of this diary. "Burn it," he would say, and I have little doubt that he is right. I love Jetty too. Her receptiveness, responsiveness, and funniness charm me. I enjoyed London — the stucco streets in the mist, with a great red sun in the fog. I liked meeting chaps for lunch in clubs and taking women out to restaurants and all the comings and goings, encounters, and gossips of London life.

March 17, 1956

One of the drearier diplomatic days. Went to the St. Patrick's Day reception at the Irish Embassy, a cheerless and squalid party unworthy of Ireland. A pile of dried old shamrocks for the guests, looking like a garbage heap, stout and watered Irish whisky to drink, and no warmth in the welcome. Dined at the Belgian Embassy. The new Ambassador and his wife have made it magnificent, the only Embassy with any style in Bonn. The dinner party had no spark. Afterwards we sat islanded in little groups in the enormous rooms. First I bored the Greek Ambassadress, then I told two long and boring stories to some people on a sofa. Then we talked about why dentists become dentists. The Portuguese Ambassador talked about Goa, and we came home.

Every middle-class German in every city is this morning starting out with his briefcase clasped firmly in his hand, wearing his long mackintosh or belted leather coat, off for his week's work, and through the half-ruined, half-rebuilt streets of the German cities goes an army of workers of all classes. The whole of Germany is like a vast school with no idle boys in it. Here everyone obeys the rules, no one protests. They cut down the only charm of Bonn—the noble trees lining the streets. There is no protest. People try to make the best of it and say, "It is *brighter* now." Brighter indeed!

April 22, 1956

Spent the whole day working on my telegram to Ottawa about the German situation and afterwards read it to Sylvia, something I never do with political dispatches. She seemed far from enthusiastic. I know it is not clear and interesting enough to hold her attention, but I despair of making it more so without over-simplifying. I sympathize with political journalists who try to make things report-able and interesting and keep them true. I think that most get to a point when they don't want to know any more about the subject. They have decided on the line they are going to take in their articles and it is confusing and encumbering to learn something new which does not fit into the picture. My trouble is a little different. I find it hard to recommend a policy except under pressure. I cannot construct in a void, and our relations with Germany are almost a void. I left off writing and went for a solitary walk when I met my friend Admiral Campbell-Walter, R.N., who has some ill-defined naval job here. He was very red in the face from celebrating the christening of one of his ratings' children. I like him very much. He is a kind of male ex-beauty, very handsome and with many conquests to his credit. He began early to learn the arts of love from Queen Marie of Romania when he was a young naval lieutenant.

Blair Fraser, the Canadian journalist, was here the other day. He is courageous, honest, and intelligent. He thinks that the Liberals are in trouble in Canada and that they will lose the election. They have depended for much of their influence on the support of a small group of publicists, professors, civil servants, and men of influence, and it is this group whose support they have lately lost.

June 5, 1956

The aunts are again staying with us—Elsie much older but still wonderful, Beatrice ageless and clear in the head but with some strange words. For instance, she says she was "dumb struck" and that someone was "criss-crossed" instead of "double-crossed". On June 2 we went over to Groesbeek Cemetery in Holland for the dedication by the Duke of Gloucester of the Canadian part of the cemetery where John Rowley is buried. It was a sunny day. The cemetery looked almost cheerful on one of the few hills in Holland. The Duke of Gloucester, very pink in the face, with popping azure eyes and wearing across his uniform the azure ribbon of the Garter, read a speech from a piece of paper held in very shaky white-gloved hands. Afterwards when I was presented to him he mumbled, "I didn't know there were so many [inaudible] around here." I couldn't think what the missing word could have been—graves? Canadians?—so I judged it safer to make no reply.

June 8, 1956

Today there was a very large and very mixed-up lunch party at our house, assembled together for the old Pells. Old Pell is an American diplomat, retired. He looks like an American senator and comes from a "grand American family". His wife is a full-busted seventy, with a lace shawl and a cupid's-bow mouth incongruously painted on a Republican lady's face. She is fond of old English music-hall songs, believes in yoga, eats no meat, and considers that all American husbands are unfaithful with women younger than their wives. All American divorces are, according to her, caused by American husbands playing on their wives' strong maternal instincts to release them from the bonds of matrimony so that they can remarry younger wives. "The American success woman is a myth. If you could only see into their hearts," she said, "you would know that they are hiding the scars inflicted on them by mainly immature and worthless American men." The new Australian Ambassadress attempted several times to interrupt by quoting U.N. statistics on divorce which proved something — just what, I never could make out. Later in the day little Del Dongo came to dinner, a nice Hungarian refugee whom I befriended in Canada, a sort of grown-up Catholic choirboy. He brought with him Father Heim from the Papal Nunciature, a shy Swiss priest who is writing a book on ecclesiastic heraldry and whose brandy glass broke in his hands after dinner. God and the Catholic Church know whether they enjoyed themselves, but they ate and drank willingly.

June 16, 1956

My usual business lunch with Von Welk. What is developing between us is as near to friendship as I have had with any German man and a sort of mutual trust, but with a misunderstood word it could crack up. Today he was very critical of Adenauer, much more openly so than he would have dared to be a short time ago. Altogether the Germans are getting more and more articulate and bold in what they say, as the Occupation recedes.

Dined with the Jakopps, German business people who live around the corner from us here in Cologne. She is plump and might be sentimental, wore a sort of handcuff of diamonds and emeralds. The German women began talking among themselves about the privations and adventures of the years just after the war, 1946-7, telling anecdotes about the shortages, how if they were asked to a reception by foreigners they would try to eat everything in sight because they were so hungry; how they would share one cigarette among a group of them, passing it around the circle; how if they had to make a journey they got lifts in coal trucks. All this was not said in a self-pitying vein or with bitterness — at times as if it seemed funny in retrospect. It shows how much safer, more prosperous, more sure of themselves the Germans are, that they can talk in this way. I must stop writing this diary now as Karl has come in to say, "Tea is served." Anyway, it is only a sort of acknowledgment for a day of life to write the diary at all, a "bread-and-butter" to God but one that must more often bore than please Him. How often the human race must bore God. I picture a cosmic yawn and His self-question, "Was it worth while creating them?"

June 18, 1956

Yesterday was wrecked for me by the discovery that the dentist had put a gold tooth in my mouth. Of all things in this world I abominate it is the gleam of a gold-toothed smile, so today I went back to the dentist again and demanded that he begin all over and make it silver. He was crimson with irritation and mortification at this reflection on his skilful work on the ambassadorial teeth, but in the end he promised to change it. God, to think that I should end up bald, with gold teeth and hairs coming out of my nose!

June 23, 1956

Still the same sunless summer. We have passed through midsummer's day without a sunny day. The visit of the Minister of Economic Affairs of Ontario has been a diversion, although an unlikely one. This "little Napoleon" has enlivened us for the last two days by his absurdities. Mistrusting me by instinct as representing the federal authorities, he has treated me throughout with unctuous politeness while bullying and insulting the junior members of the Embassy staff. Yesterday I had a reception for him of German bankers and businessmen.

The Minister arrived an hour late, when the Germans were just on the point of departure. The old aunts have left to go home to Canada and we shall miss them. They bring a breath of spontaneity and fun into the stuffiest gathering, and Elsie, even deaf and ill at seventy-eight, has more heart and vitality than most of the people I know and I really love her.

June 29, 1956 — London

Spent the day with Mike Pearson and the Prime Minister and discussed European policy questions and Canada's relationship to them with Mike. The Prime Minister seems sunk in melancholia. He certainly appears to find no fun or interest in politics and perhaps he had better get out of it.

July 12, 1956 — Cologne

My cousin Wilfred Ponsonby is staying here from England. He and Lance Pope were talking as we lunched on a sunny terrace on the Rhine about their exploits when they were prisoners of war in Germany — of getting over the wire, of the brilliant but abortive escape when Lance got out dressed as a German general in a uniform made in camp, only to be caught a few hours later while changing in a nearby wood into civilian clothes. But mostly they talked about tunnels — the incredible feats of engineering, concealment, and patience which went into the digging of these tunnels by underfed prisoners suffering from the lassitude of malnutrition, and how, after months of digging, on the day before the big break-out they were given away to the Germans by a spy in the camp. All day I have been thinking about this kind of staying power, this continuous bending of all energies and ingenuity to the idea of escape and the techniques of achieving it, the turning of everything to one purpose. In the afternoon to an odious reception, mostly Baltic barons and their county wives. Talked to one woman who, when I asked her if she liked Bonn, said, "Wherever *mein Mann* is, there I am happy." I nearly laughed in her face.

At this point the developing crisis over the Suez Canal began to overshadow the international scene. As there are so many references in the following diaries to Suez, it may be helpful briefly to recall the history of those events which not only altered the balance of power in the world but affected relations between individuals and led to such bitter and divided personal feelings.

The seizure of the Suez Canal by President Nasser of Egypt in July 1956 led to the intervention by the British and French to retake the Canal. The plan worked out at secret meetings with the Israelis was for Israel to attack Egypt, and then the British and French would go in, ostensibly to separate the combatants. On October 29, Israeli forces crossed the frontier and captured Egyptian border posts, and by November 5 British and French paratroopers landed in Port Said, to be followed by the arrival of ships carrying the main assault forces.

These developments caused consternation in the United Nations, in Washington, and in Ottawa. L. B. Pearson, then Minister of External Affairs, went to the United Nations in New York. He was shocked at the action of the British Prime Minister, Anthony Eden, in sanctioning an enterprise which would antagonize the Arab world, split the Commonwealth, and put such a strain on Anglo-American relations. The idea of a United Nations Emergency Force was not a new one but it was his initiative and his diplomatic skill that brought it into being. Throughout, he worked in close co-operation with the Secretary-General, Dag Hammarskjöld. The United Nations Force was intended to proceed to the Suez Canal area on the withdrawal of the Anglo-French expedition.

On November 4 the Canadian resolution setting up the Force was introduced in the United Nations General Assembly by L. B. Pearson and approved by the Assembly.

Meanwhile, the U.S.S.R. was occupied in crushing the two-weeks-old Hungarian people's rebellion. Now they proposed that the United Nations give military assistance to Egypt. When the Security Council refused to discuss this proposal, the Russians addressed threatening Notes to the United Kingdom, France, and Israel. On November 6 the Franco-British invasion of the Suez Canal Zone was halted when Prime Minister Eden agreed to a cease-fire in view of the formation of the United Nations Emergency Force, of the United States' opposition to the operation, and of a heavy run on the pound sterling. So this ill-conceived venture ended in humiliating failure and the subsequent resignation of Prime Minister Eden on grounds of ill health. In England the role played by Canada in this whole affair aroused mixed feelings. On the surface there was appreciation of the fact that Pearson had helped the British out of an increasingly impossible situation. Yet there was also resentment at the lack of Canadian approval and support for the United Kingdom government. The Prime Minister, Mr. St. Laurent, had indeed made a public statement extremely critical of the United Kingdom and of France. Canadian opinion was divided; the Conservative Opposition launched a bitter attack on the government, claiming that they had sided with Nasser and the United States against Britain and France. The government's handling of the Suez crisis may have had some effect on the 1957 election, which brought the Conservatives to power for the first time in twenty-two years. Thus Pearson was out of office when he received the Nobel Peace Prize for his contribution to peace-keeping. With the change of government in 1957 and the arrival in office of the Diefenbaker administration, Pearson was succeeded as Secretary of State for External Affairs by Sidney Smith, who in turn was succeeded in 1959 by Howard Green.

September 14, 1956

The shadow of the Suez crisis is over everything, so perhaps this little Bonn world does not look so bad when war might threaten its disappearance. Could we really be headed for another war, or only the humiliation of all that is left of Britain's greatness? Is it to be a bang or a whimper? The weakness of the British position is that people do not believe in their shopworn phrases such as "free men everywhere" and "world opinion". The point is that "free men everywhere" are far from convinced that the principle of freedom is endangered by Nasser as they knew it was by Hitler.

September 15, 1956 — Battle of Britain Sunday

I do wish the English would stop saying that the choice is between war and their having to pay one and sixpence more for a gallon of petrol because it would have to come around the Cape, because this argument cannot make them many converts.

We went to the Battle of Britain Sunday service in the little RAF church here and had gin and tonic afterwards on the lawn of the RAF Mess with the Air Vice-Marshal, who thinks there will be a war and blames it on the Foreign Office. Spent the afternoon reading the Sunday papers about Suez until I could read no more and turned to the *Towers of Trebizond* by Rose Macaulay.

September 16, 1956

A break from the crisis in the form of a visit to Bonn by the King and Queen of Greece. There was a reception for them last night at Schloss Bruhl. * Quite a spectacle. The royal procession leaving between a bowing row of guests looked like an early movie of court life in old Vienna. Schloss Bruhl was lighted with candelabra wreathed in roses. The rococo décor had all been renewed and looked theatrical. There were striped marquees in the candle-lit gardens and music "off". There was a touch of Balkan royalty about the uniforms of the Greek court officials. I shook hands with the manager of the hotel responsible for the catering and said, "Good evening, Your Excellency," mistaking him for one of my obscurer colleagues. He looked profoundly gratified. The Soviet Chargé d'Affaires came to me (why me?) and said, "Can I go home now?" like a little boy. I said severely, "No, the King and Queen are still here and you cannot leave until they go." He looked quite desperate.

October 7, 1956

Just back from spending the night in Wiesbaden with Sylvia. Down the Rhine road in a mixture of rain and shafts of sunlight, weather which suits the poetic and dramatic style. Lunched in a restaurant under an old castle on a crag above a village, the village decked with flags for the Weinfest. Drank thin, sour, ice-cold wine and went on a tour of the castle, now a museum. The horrid life lived in that castle by those medieval troglodytes in armour; the small, dank, dark, slit-eyed rooms into which they crowded! The Ritterhall was full of armoured figures and one imagined the echo of the brutish laughter of these sinister iron robots who, once unarmoured, must have thronged around the fireplace roasting an ox or a disobedient serf. It was a giant's lair from a frightening fairy tale, a place for tortures, with dungeons deep in the rock. In the

*The eighteenth-century palace outside Cologne used by the German government for official entertainment.

museum hangs a bearded mask with openings for eyes. This was made red-hot and pressed over the victim's face; also the first chastity belt I have seen — a thin opening in the iron which nothing substantial could penetrate and a hoop around the body, the key given to the butler and only to be opened if the husband did not return from the Crusades after three years. Down we came from this dismal place and when I saw in the Wiesbaden Gallery the portrait of a young knight in ornamented Renaissance armour with a fair killer's face, there in the background was just such a Rhine castle on a crag. I thought of those proud whelps being engendered in the dark curtained bed in that top turret chamber behind the thick stone walls with the slit-eyed view down the precipitous tower wall to the broad Rhine flowing between swelling hills. Wiesbaden after this was a welcome return to civilization. I like these German watering-places as well as anything in Germany. They have an agreeable touch of cosmopolitanism. The hotels are good, even luxurious. They can make a decent martini at the bar. The water is boiling hot in the baths. It is pleasant to stroll through the arcades of the casino or to walk along the allées in the garden. We mildly gambled and ate partridge cooked in the German style with sauerkraut and grapes, which made Sylvia feel sick.

October 8, 1956
    A visit from a German diplomat concerned with Canada, a large, florid gentleman who emanated scent and appeared to me to be suffering from a hangover, not taking it quietly but trying to override it, thus giving the impression of too much manner. He had uneasy hazel eyes, a faint trace of a duelling scar across his pink cheek, and heavy white hands emerging from cream-coloured silk cuffs worn rather long in the English manner. He was certainly in no condition to discuss the Air Training Programme or any other Canadian-German question. Later Aga Fürsten-

burg came in for one of our absurd German lessons. We are reading a Simenon detective story in German but she interrupts the whole time to gossip in English. She is very good company but my German is not progressing. I had been told how after the assassination plot against Hitler she had hidden two of the plotters in her apartment in Berlin. I asked her how she got away with it and why she was not suspected. She said, "The Nazis never did take me seriously." Perhaps that was the best protective colouring in that jungle.

I am becoming attached to Aga. She now gives me lessons three times a week. We had met at the house of mutual friends who heard my complaints about the German teachers I have hired up till now and, knowing that she could do with the extra money, suggested her name to me. From the moment that she strolled into my office for the first lesson, I might have known that all serious hope of my mastering the German language had vanished. Aga must be about my own age — in the late forties; tall, leggy, she resembles a giraffe, with a giraffe's expression of absent-minded *hauteur*. This is her first experience of teaching and she has a novel approach to the subject. "What has prevented you from learning German better," she says, "is boredom. You will never learn if you are bored. So don't bother with the grammar. What do you read to relax?" "Simenon," I replied. "Good. I like him very much myself — we'll start with him." "But he writes in French." "That doesn't matter. His books are translated into German. You shall have your copy and I mine. We shall· read together — you will translate the German into English as we go along, with my corrections, of course." This system, if it can be called a system, is not working very effectively, as Aga is always breaking into my laborious translating with some startling and scandalous story of life in Berlin under the Nazis when she was employed in some ill-defined capacity in the Foreign Office, or the private lives of our Bonn acquaintance. Her stories, told in a mixture of French, German, and English, often leave the solid ground of fact and leap into the upper air of fantastic fun and cruel wit. When inspiration fails she sinks back on the sofa, opens her handbag, and, extracting a small brown bottle of Unterberg, takes a sip of it and with a sigh turns back to Simenon. (I have myself experimented with Unterberg, the German health drink or pick-me-up — a noxious concoction with quite a kick to it.)

Aga comes of an aristocratic Westphalian family. A brother with whom she is on quarrelling terms now lives in the family schloss, but her grown-up life was spent in Berlin and one can see traces in her of the hectic, sophisticated, despairing Berlin of the twenties when she was young. When the Russians entered Berlin she came as a refugee to Bonn. She has one deep attachment from the Berlin years — Baron Zetsé Pfuel. Like her, he has a record of anti-Nazi courage. He and Aga give the impression of having seen both better and worse times together, and of having been cast up on these shores after the storms of their lives had subsided, leaving them empty of any future. I find Zetsé an attractive figure, with his striking looks and his high spirits which can change quickly to gloom. Like Aga, he has a reckless tongue. Through them I have met some of the refugees from East Prussia and Berlin — they bring with them a whiff of cynical wit and debunking frankness quite different from the Rhinelanders. They form a little world of their own in Bonn, crowded into small, shabby apartments, having escaped with nothing; taking odd jobs where they can find them and free meals from their Rhineland friends and relations. They remind me of the White Russian refugees I knew in my youth.

Aga surprised me the other day with a sudden outburst — "Why do you people pretend to sympathize with us Germans in wanting reunification of Germany? What a farce! We all know that that is the last thing you want.

Why should you want a bigger Germany? Of course you don't trust us. Why should you? Why pretend?" I was on the point of protesting, but to do so would be an insult to her intelligence. I said nothing. The silence marks our mutual understanding and its limits.

October 31, 1956 — Halifax, Nova Scotia

I am here on a visit home to see my mother and today I have been walking the streets of the town. Halifax has lost its peculiar flavour of a nineteenth-century garrison town and its look of faded gentility. For a long time people used to say that the citizens of Halifax never painted their houses but let them look shabbier and shabbier to avoid high tax assessments. That reproach can never be uttered again. People have gone hog-wild with the paintbrush and the houses have blossomed out in pinks and greens and pastel shades. Rather touching to see these old-fashioned houses having another fling at life, but so many places that used to be gardens are now Esso stations.

The day of my "coronation", * as my mother calls it. Why did I ever get involved in giving this address, particularly in the Cathedral, where I am to make a speech to — among others — the King's College students? The speech itself is a respectable collection of second-hand ideas expressed in the usual clichés. As I walked across the old golf links, following a path I used to take on my way to King's College when I was a student there, I thought of what I should be saying to these young men. "Don't be taken in by vain old buffers like me. Escape if you can from the terrifying conventionality of this atmosphere. Don't be trapped by fear or affection into conforming over anything that matters." I looked among the students I saw on their way to the Cathedral for a bespectacled, self-conscious, angular youth — for myself when young — but they all

*I had been awarded an honorary D.C.L. by my old University of King's College.

looked very free and easy and neither self-conscious nor angular.

November 6, 1956

The international situation is taking on a nightmare aspect. Mr. St. Laurent says that the Soviet ultimatum to the United Kingdom does not make him tremble in his boots. That is as may be, but I must get back to Bonn at once. I cannot be caught in Halifax at a time like this, not that my presence in Bonn will make the slightest difference to anything.

November 13, 1956 — London

I hate being in London when so much is at stake for the English and when I do not feel at one with them. I am haunted by memories of 1940 when I felt such a complete identity with the Londoners. It seems like a desertion on my part and no doubt many of my friends here think that it is a desertion of them on the part of Canada. Elizabeth Bowen says, "What if we *are* wrong? If one of my friends made a mistake or committed a crime I would back them up. It is as simple as that." She has a raging contempt for the U.N. and its moral palaver. I said to Michael the other night, "It is not that I am troubled by the so-called immorality of the Suez action, it is just a question of what the international traffic will bear or will not bear and our assessment is different from yours." But feeling runs high and one has to be careful even with one's friends. Anne said to me, "Don't desert England — how can you?"

November 18, 1956 — Cologne

Three o'clock on Sunday afternoon, the hour of my birth and always the lowest point in the week for me; the inexpressibly melancholy sound of voices drifting up to the window from the foggy suburban street. I am trying to go over and over in my mind this beastly Suez affair so that I can decide on the line to take in talking to my diplomatic colleagues and to the Germans. It is one thing to criticize the English to their faces or to my fellow Canadians. It is quite another thing to criticize them before foreigners and before those who hate them. My friend the Admiral came in this morning for a drink. We were both very careful in discussing Suez to keep unemotional for fear of another row between us over politics, and he kept on calling me "Charles" affectionately to show that there was "no offence" after our last argument. I would have reciprocated if I could have remembered his first name. Derek Hoyer-Miller (the British Ambassador) very nice, very friendly and understanding of our position.

November 21, 1956

Today is Repentance Day in Germany and a holiday. I don't know what they are repenting — they have plenty to choose from. Sylvia and I went for a walk this afternoon in the grounds of Schloss Bruhl. It was a fine, clear early winter's day, the last roses frozen and the walks in the park carpeted with bronze leaves. I came back to read the English papers and felt sick at heart at the pass to which British prestige has been brought, and divided between my certainty that their government's policy has been a colossal, disastrous blunder and my emotional sympathy for the English, particularly when isolated and when so many are turning against them. Today the servants found a revolver behind the wall in an upstairs room in this house. It has been lying there since street fighting when the Allied troops fought their way into Cologne. Perhaps a German soldier had thrown it there to get rid of it.

Called on Couve* and found him very objective over Suez. (By that I really mean that he agreed with me.) But he did say that the situation in France is different from that

---

*Couve de Murville, the French Ambassador. He succeeded François-Poncet and was later Foreign Minister of France.

in England because in France "we are all involved; the whole population except the Communist Party and a few isolated individuals are in favour of our action over Suez." I again reflected how little like a Frenchman Couve is, with his reserved, cool manner and his English clothes, but perhaps the difference is only skin deep or perhaps it is because he is a Protestant.

November 25, 1956

Another Sunday. Went to the RAF Chapel across the street which is really just the upper room of a house very much like this one. The Welsh clergyman read with beautiful, unaffected appreciation the lesson from Ecclesiastes, "Remember now thy Creator", etc. The mournful majesty of it echoed disturbingly around the room. It makes most of the Old Testament prophets sound like angry old men shouting their terrible denunciations and shrieks for vengeance. The clergyman preached against sloth. The congregation of young men sang vigorously. This is called "stirring-up" Sunday.

I hope that in Ottawa they realize that the time has come to help to save the face of the British over Suez. The British will be there long after Eden has gone and will remain the best bet in a bad world. They should not be humiliated, and Canada should be the first to see that. I hope that we are not too much influenced by unreal majorities of the United Nations. As for the Russian ultimatum, shall we yet see Russian tanks rumbling through the surburban streets of Cologne on some such dark Sunday afternoon as this, and where then will be our complaints about being bored?

November 27, 1956

Lunched with the diplomatic colleagues. An endless discussion over protocol. If you are giving a dinner "in honour" of someone, is it possible to put the wife of the guest of honour on the right-hand side of the host — in other words, higher up than invited Ambassadresses? The answer of most of the colleagues is "No, it would be grossly improper." The Italian Ambassador has sent members of the Diplomatic Corps an invitation to dinner for the President of Italy, who is visiting Bonn, but he has sent it in the name of the President instead of in his own name. The question arises whether a Head of State can issue invitations when he is on foreign soil or whether it must be his Ambassador who does this.

By tacit agreement, Suez and events in Hungary are not discussed in a diplomatic group of this kind, but only between pairs of individual ambassadors, to avoid emotional rows.

The Yugoslav Ambassador called, an intelligent man more interested in politics than in protocol. He is bitterly disappointed by the turn of events in Hungary but he is more anxious to blame the West than the Russians.

November 30, 1956

In the evening, dinner at the Campbell-Walters'. My host, the Admiral, was in a melancholy and silent mood but Mrs. Campbell-Walter more than made up for it. Their daughter, the beautiful Fiona, was there with her new husband, the millionaire Heinie Thyssen. She was wearing the famous great pearl which he has given her and which has had so much publicity in the press. Fiona is that rare article, a real beauty — not just pretty or handsome or attractive, but a Beauty. She combines this with very quick wits. She is very unselfconscious about her looks. I thought of how the greatest beauty of them all, Diana Cooper, talks of "the face" as if it were not part of her but a valuable possession which had to be taken care of. Heinie Thyssen's attitude towards Fiona always seems to me to be that of a connoisseur who has added to his collection rather than that of a lover. He has indeed collected at least one earlier decorative wife in addition to so many superb works of art. Fiona's younger sister Sheila was there. She is a pert, funny girl and greeted me by saying, "How are you, you old whisky-slinger?"

Reading Beckford's diaries. They are very fascinating reading but *any* diary has a certain fascination for me, even the most trivial ones. We are buying another dog, this time a Schnauzer. We thought a little brother might be good for Popski, whose ego is getting completely out of hand. The only trouble is that I suspect that this new puppy is a "disturbed personality". He has a very mad look in his eye.

Tonight we are giving a dance in honour of Roger Rowley's daughter Andrea, who is eighteen. Everything has been left to the last moment. At this very moment workmen are pulling up half the loose tiles in the dance floor and hammering in some new ones. They say they will cover them with some quick-drying cement that will dry in an hour, but I picture it sticking to the shoes of the dancers and rooting them to the floor — a motionless ball. Then "they" sent only half-bottles of champagne, so that there is only half enough, so that we are involved in an illicit deal with the French Club — but will the champagne be here in time for the dance? We have asked far too many people for the size of the house. It is a physical impossibility for 110 people to dance in that hall, and still acceptances are coming in, including people who are not on any of the lists. Who the hell, for example, is Lord Chelsea? I think it must be a spoof name.

December 1, 1956

The dance seems to have been a great success. It certainly went on long enough. I got so exhausted at one point that I retired to the W.C. and sat there reading Beckford's diaries with a whisky in my hand. The door unexpectedly opened and two of the girl guests came in. They gazed at me in horror and amazement and fled.

There is a ridiculous flurry in the German socialist press today against the Canadian Army, saying that a Canadian soldier bit the ear off a German in Dortmund during a row over parking a car. The press have been after me on the telephone about it, one journalist asking me if I could make "an educated guess" as to what had really happened.

January 19, 1957

Back from Ireland after staying with Elizabeth at Bowen's Court. Got into a conversation on the plane with a young Irishman who was returning from London to live in his native County Cork. He said, "You get tired of the city, but in the country there is nothing to get tired of." I pondered this elliptical remark.

How can one convey the fascinating flow of Elizabeth's talk, the pictures of places and people, the continual surprise and pleasure of her choice of a word, the funniness, poetry, and near-brutality of her view of a situation? One day we went off to the wedding of the daughter of the farmer who lives by the gate of Bowen's Court and who was marrying a young man who has a shop and runs the post office in Kilmallock. The very young bridegroom was as pale as ashes. After the wedding the bride and groom were photographed standing in the church porch and off we drove to the wedding breakfast in a country hotel twenty miles away. There were clans of Hodginses and Harrises, all "strong farmers", all Protestant. Their Catholic friends who could not go to the church stood at their doors in Kildorrery village and waved the bridal party a send-off. At the wedding breakfast I sat next to old Aunt Hodgins, toothless but talkative. We spoke of Life and she said, with a sidelong glance at me out of her bright blue eyes, "And what are we all hoping for?" There was Irish whisky and champagne and a speech from the eighteen-year-old best man, a country boy, in which he compared the bridesmaid to the Queen of Sheba.

On another day we drove over to Muckross. Elizabeth said of that wild, steamy, strange County Kerry country that it suggested temperament, with an unexplained, unreasoning flash of joy followed by darkling, curdling weather when the lakes turned from sunny blue to black. She showed me some of the Bowen topography, the scenes where some of her short stories are placed.

Elizabeth says that her next book is to be called *A Race with Time*. She says that she knows its title but not yet exactly what it is to be about. There will be a "star-shaped" plot with characters and events converging on a point in time. She is working very hard at her present book, writing all morning on most days and in the early afternoon. She says that when a woman becomes a widow she goes back to the arts and crafts of her youth in attaching friends and combining people and, in order not to be lonely, returns to her earlier gregariousness.

Talking of writing she said, "I could give a very good vivid description of the road past Headington where I used to walk every day, but who would want to read it unless something happened there?" She says that she does not want to write a subjective autobiography. She wants to invent, or rather that it comes more naturally to her to invent.

February 19, 1957

I have excluded from these diaries almost any reference to office work or mention of members of the Embassy staff or descriptions of any official business or negotiations with the German government. I have absolutely no wish to write about such things, which anyway are covered by memoranda and dispatches in the office. Then there is another consideration — security. I have always been almost excessively "security-minded". In addition, this house is full of German servants of varied backgrounds. Then Bonn is, I think, riddled with spies of different persuasions. The result of all this is that the diaries have a very unbalanced look as though I were a man of leisure who did nothing but go to parties and never did a day's work. The truth is that I very much like office work and very much enjoy the transaction of business. Indeed, my main complaint about this post is that there is not enough business to transact. As a result of leaving out any political or diplomatic record the diaries would be of less interest to readers, but this does not matter as I do not intend that there should be any readers. I have provided in my will that all my papers should be destroyed at my death. Why then do I write the diaries? It is a compulsion, like smoking.

February 21, 1957

I went over today to Dortmund to open an exhibition of Eskimo art. I have already opened three exhibitions of Eskimo art and am becoming sick of the sight of it. This exhibition was in the museum at Dortmund and the museum officials had told me that they had very few funds to provide refreshments, so I sent over several cases of rye whisky. The people at the museum had never seen rye before and the Director asked me if it was "a kind of liqueur or a sort of wine". After the speeches were over, tall glasses filled with undiluted rye whisky were handed round on trays and drunk recklessly, so that before the reception was over everyone was more or less drunk. It was by far the most successful exhibition of Eskimo art I have ever attended, although towards the end of the evening things got somewhat out of control. A German art critic came to me and said that he knew that the Eskimo objects were not genuine but were copies made in Germany of objects sculptured by a German sculptor called Arndt. However, he promised that he would not reveal this in the article he wrote in tomorrow's paper about the exhibition. I could not convince him that he was mistaken. He went on repeating in a drunken fashion, "I promise not to tell, Your Excellency, I promise not to tell," until two tears began to run down his cheeks. One of the senior officials in the museum was a large, masculine lady with a broad, noble forehead, wearing on her finger an outsize signet ring. She seemed strongly attracted by a chinless young woman from the Cultural Division of the Foreign Office and they ended in a warm embrace and the promise that they would spend the evening together. The reception ended with group photographs which I shall certainly treasure.

I had a letter today from Anne in which she wrote to me of the time when we were young in the twenties. Few of my contemporaries, male or female, married young. She was an exception. In those days we would have thought it a premature descent into the dreary world of middle-aged domesticity. As politics did not interest us, nor religion nor money unless it fell into our laps, we must now wonder what did interest that generation. I can only speak for myself. I was after Experience. I lived in the private conviction that intense, strongly poetic, dramatic Experience lay in wait for me. I longed for a condition in which reality lived up to literature. Meanwhile I did little to bring this state about. I was a "mirror dawdling down a lane", but I was a talking mirror. I only loved solitude when I knew that company was round the corner.

As I was thinking of those days a scene swam into my mind. It is Paris, some time in the twenties. Here is a random group of friends and acquaintances picked up in night-clubs, joy-rides in borrowed cars, and casual couplings. We had all been together for days and nights, spin-

ning about the town in a nonsensical saraband, intox-
icated with our own youth and with the cocktails of the
time — Alexanders, Sidecars, White Ladies. Now we
stood drinking, talking, and laughing together in some
bar, making a noise, showing off, under the eyes of a
disapproving couple of men who are quietly shooting dice
in a corner of the bar. (That is what we wanted, dis-
approval and attention — insufferable and enjoyable
behaviour.) There was Basil, the enfranchised son of a
rural dean, a rubber-faced joker and lecher; Jo from Mis-
souri, a bright-eyed, solemn girl who knew better but
wanted to savour dissipation in Paris; a silent, wooden
Scottish textile millionaire in a checked jacket; a pale,
plump White Russian who could do card tricks and was
employed in the perfume business; and of course Lavinia,
skinny, flat-chested, lovely long legs, hyperthyroid eyes,
skirts to her knees, the Lady Lavinia, a lost lady in the
Michael Arlen fashion, a Bright Young Thing now a
trifle tarnished, heroine of endless escapades, figuring in
a fashionable novel. Her gaiety now gone a trifle shrill,
her wit blurred with drink, yet eager for enjoyment, she
could still spark a party. There was a gramophone in this
American bar and we kept pestering the bartender for our
favourite tunes, moaning jazz laments, "Sweet Chee-ild,
You're Driving Me Crazy" — the tunes of futility and
longing.

February 22, 1957
    I have been seeing a great deal of Brentano, the
German Foreign Minister, in the last weeks. We seem to
get on rather well and this may prove useful. I am beginning to speak German quite fluently but only social German. I never speak it when I go to the Foreign Office. It is
very risky to do business in a foreign language and my
German is certainly not up to it. Even in "social" German I

mistrust myself for fear of giving just the wrong emphasis, greater intimacy than I feel, a cruder judgement than I intend, or just a joke that does not come off.

March 17, 1957

Went to the airport to meet Sylvia on her return from Canada. What my life would be without her I cannot imagine. She was so sweet and looking beautiful. She rises to all occasions, never fusses or nags. I am a lucky man and I know it.

April 5, 1957

I have a spring cold in the head and the spring goes on without me. This morning began badly by my throwing a ball for Popski which scored a direct hit on one of the china urns which we bought in Marseilles. It came crashing onto the black and white stone tiles of the hall, making a splendid row.

In the afternoon a German in jackboots came to see me. He has been pestering me for an interview for days. He says that he has been wrongly arrested by the Canadian police as a former Nazi, whereas he claims that he was only a driver in a transport division. He stood very straight and it was a question whether in his emotional state he would hit me on the head with a blunt instrument or burst into sobs. I felt sad and weary for his desperation and I gave him ten marks. His battered pride moved me. He probably should have been shot long ago and would get scant sympathy from his fellow Germans. Karl, the butler, said, "Yes, he was lucky before in the Nazi days. Now things are not good for him. What does he expect?"

I wonder whether the Air Attaché should have given my secretary a book called *The Strangler in the House of Lust*, with illustrations.

June 23, 1957

Zetsé Pfuel, Aga's friend, told me last night that he and his wife had escaped from Berlin on the last train which left for the West when the Russians had already entered the city. He said that on the morning of their departure his wife informed him that she was going out to have her hair done. He protested and said that it was very likely that she would never get back through Berlin to the station in time for departure and that the Russian troops were moving into the centre of the city. She said, "If you think that I am going to stay with your rich cousins in the Rhineland and arrive at their house as a poor refugee with my hair straggling down my back you are very much mistaken." Zetsé then went back to his Ministry, burned various files, and went to the station where his wife was to join him. He said he never put in such an agonizing hour as the hour he spent waiting for her. She arrived exactly two minutes before the departure of the last train, with her hair done.

Then the talk turned to life in Germany during the war. One couple who had a country house in Westphalia said that, while they were not Nazis, they went along with the régime. There was nothing else that they could do. The garage proprietor in the neighbouring village was a Nazi official. All the villagers were under his control. If they had not kept on good terms with him it would have been impossible for them to buy anything in the village. As it was, their lack of enthusiasm was already suspected and they were treated with great coolness by the local people. If they had openly opposed the régime they would have been at once deported to a concentration camp. This had already happened to their cousins in the neighbour-hood. They said that most people knew something of the horrors of the concentration camps but by no means every-thing. It was very dangerous to try to find out any more, as

the only result would be to land up in one of the camps
oneself. I often wonder whether we Canadians would have
been much more willing than the Germans to defy Hitler
once the country was in his power.

January 5, 1958
    A few months ago when we were coming back from
the weekend in Paris and the train was coming in to
Cologne station, I looked out at the bulk of the Cathedral
looming against the grey evening sky and found myself
saying, "We are home again." How inconceivable it
would have seemed to me, nearly four years ago when we
came here, ever to have this feeling of familiarity verging
on affection for this place and these people. One senses in
the Germans a controlled neurosis, admires the control
and mistrusts the neurosis. They have such immense
potentialities for achievement and such a contribution to
make to Europe. They are like a friend of whom one could
say, "He will go far if he does not go too far."

New York

In January 1958 I took up my new appointment as Permanent Representative of Canada to the United Nations. During that year Canada was a member of the Security Council and I served a term as President of the Security Council. I remained at the United Nations from 1958 to 1962.

When I arrived in New York in 1958 it was as the representative of a country well-known as a strong supporter of the United Nations. Mike Pearson, the former Minister of External Affairs, had been the embodiment of this policy. With the coming to power of the Conservative government in 1957 there was no falling off in Canadian support for the United Nations, which was backed up by widespread favourable opinion in the country. The Conservative ministers of External Affairs, first Sidney Smith and then, in 1959, Howard Green, were active in United Nations affairs. Howard Green devoted much of his time and energy to the United Nations and, in particular, to the cause of disarmament. The position of Canadian Permanent Representative to the United Nations was thus considered by the government to be an important one. I had had a fairly extensive experience of the United Nations since 1945, when I had been an Advisor to the Canadian Delegation to the San Francisco Conference, which founded the Organization. Since then I had served as Advisor, Observer, or Alternate Delegate at a series of sessions of the General Assembly and the Security Council and I had taken an active part in United Nations disarmament negotiations. I looked forward to the pressures and excitement of my new job and to the change of scene from Bonn to New York, and I was not disappointed. The years I spent at the United Nations were the most stimulating, if sometimes the most frustrating, of my diplomatic career.

For me the attraction of the United Nations was as a centre for international negotiation — a unique meeting-place of diverse groupings and interests and a framework for the resolution of problems or at least the papering-over of cracks and the averting of explosions. I was less impressed by the global ideology, the "one world" language of some of its more Messianic supporters, and I had few illusions about its ultimate effectiveness in peace-keeping or disarmament. I enjoyed the combination of public and private diplomacy, the open sessions of the General Assembly and the Security Council, and the long-drawn-out bargaining behind the scenes which preceded every public declaration. All of this was of absorbing professional interest to any diplomat, particularly one who like myself preferred negotiation to representation. It is true that the eons of boredom endured during speeches in the General Assembly took a heavy toll, but at least one did not have to speechify oneself. That was best left to one's political masters. Indeed, to seek — worse still to obtain — personal publicity at the United Nations is, for the career diplomat, the kiss of death. It is resented by the politicians and deplored by one's fellow members of the Service.

I had many friends among journalists accredited to the Organization. I had, in my youth, aspired to journalism and had served a turn on Beaverbrook's *London Evening Standard*. I never could understand the mistrust and alarm with which some diplomats viewed the press, for in the two-way relationship between diplomat and journalist the diplomat often has quite as much to gain as the journalist. I was to find this even more true later, when I was Ambassador in Washington. Certainly I learned more, not only in information but in wisdom, from that great man Walter Lippmann than I could ever repay, and James Reston knew more of American political life and politicians than any Ambassador could absorb in a lifetime.

Although I found the United Nations job a fascinating one, it was not good for the diaries. The attempt to combine the pace of work with the pleasures of New York meant that I had less time to write the diary regularly. I notice too, in these diaries, an increasingly caustic note. The close association with my colleagues in the hothouse atmosphere of the United Nations building, while it led to close friendships, could breed irritability. If I sometimes wrote disparagingly about my profession and its practitioners, allowances should be made for temporary exasperation. I would never myself have exchanged the diplomatic career for any other. Diplomats have never, as a group, been much loved. They are accused of many things — starchy manners and over-supple consciences, secretiveness and deviousness. In fact they are a hard-headed knowledgeable, tolerant lot, often more long-sighted than their political masters. Of course, there are joke figures among them, petty-minded and pretentious, but that is true of every occupation. As for our own Foreign Service, it stands comparison with any I have ever encountered. Certainly the men and women who worked with me at our Mission in New York were among the ablest and most-respected at the United Nations. Naturally a diplomat's effectiveness is ultimately determined by the confidence he inspires in his own government. It is sometimes supposed that there is an inbred mistrust between the permanent civil servant and the politician. Having served under five prime ministers I cannot subscribe to this notion. The worst case is the combination of a suspicious or insecure Minister and an unimaginative or smug official. Those who are safely ensconced in the permanent civil service may sometimes forget that politicians, however temporarily powerful, and at times arrogant, are always walking a tightrope of risk from which the fall is oblivion. My own sympathy tended to be with the risk-takers.

Whether or not it has proved to be a wise decision to locate the United Nations in New York, for me personally it was a happy choice. Sometimes New York tired me, but I never tired of New York. Many of our friends there neither knew nor cared anything about the United Nations; they lived in other worlds of interest and amusement. Elizabeth Bowen came on frequent visits to the United States, lecturing or as writer-in-residence at American universities, and was often in New York where she had so many friends and which she so much enjoyed, although during this time she was in the throes of a financial crisis which resulted in the sale of Bowen's Court, her beloved family home in Ireland.

Looking back upon the New York chapter of my life I still feel, as I wrote at the time, that I should make a libation of gratitude to the Goddess of Liberty at her gates. These diaries terminate with my appointment in 1962 as Ambassador to Washington, a new challenge for the diplomat and a change of scene for the diarist.

January 20, 1958 — New York

Today I presented my Letters of Credence to Dag Hammarskjöld. He twinkled at me and turned on the charm. What is he like? Modest conceit, subtlety, vanity, intimacy switched on and off, an intriguing little creature. Is he to be the "Saviour of the World"? He would probably make as good a shot at it as anyone else. He talked of Mike

Pearson, of their working so closely together at the time of the Suez crisis and the setting up of the U.N. peace-keeping force. He seems to look on Canada as a member of an inner circle — the "Scandi-Canadians" is his word — who, together with Ireland, are particularly dedicated to the United Nations and share his objectives and his point of view. He wants to get Geoff Murray, the number two in our Mission, on his own staff. I do not welcome this, as Geoff is one of the ablest operators on the U.N. scene and his experience and ability will be invaluable to me, but I suspect that Hammarskjöld will prove persistent about this. He has the reputation of taking up new people who attract his attention — and sometimes dropping them again.

In the long bar at the U.N. I met John Hood, the Australian Representative. We had three or four jumbo-sized Manhattans each. I don't know if this is the order of the day at the U.N. In the afternoon walked in Central Park — icy wind, cloudless blue sky, the wild animals shrunken in their cages, bored jaguars, comatose pumas, a wild-animal smell that hung about one for an hour afterwards. To a cocktail party in the evening. I had forgotten how much the Americans love talking on social occasions about international affairs and how earnestly distressed they are about the conduct of everyone everywhere — the French in North Africa, the Germans in Germany, the Russians, and of course the Americans themselves. "Aren't you depressed about the international situation?" as an opening gambit in conversation at a cocktail party always makes me feel like persiflage.

January 23, 1958

Entering the U.N. building is like going aboard a vast, gleaming ship moored off 42nd Street. You might have turned at the entrance to wave goodbye to the passing

New Yorkers left behind in the street, before joining the motley crowd of your fellow passengers on the voyage outward-bound — the compass pointing to far horizons — the weather uncertain, with gale warnings out — and the final destination unknowable. One after another the gleaming black Cadillacs, pennants fluttering, sweep onto the curving driveway before the great glass doors, and out step the diplomats, dapper in their dark business suits, heading for the entrance with the air of preoccupation of men who have grave matters on their minds. Following come their juniors, swinging briefcases purposefully. The uniformed guards at the front door have the business of knowing them all by sight and nation, and giving each a respectful yet friendly greeting. They do it well. The U.N. guards do everything well, from managing the mass exodus at the end of a public session to controlling the unruly in the public gallery. They are picked for strength as well as intelligence. The bartenders at the long bar know the drinking preferences of half the world. The telephone operators and the lounge receptionists can track down an Ambassador for an urgent long-distance call from his capital at any hour of the day or night. The interpreters are sophisticated, tactful, tireless artists of language. These are the indispensable crew without whom the ship would founder. They could teach a lesson in good temper and good manners to some of the delegates. An escalator leads up from the entrance to the upper level of the Assembly Hall and the Council Chambers. As one ascends one mingles with the incoming colleagues — "There is a point I should like to raise with you before the vote this afternoon. Could we meet in the usual corner in the Delegates' Lounge in half an hour?" or "Have you had a reply yet from your government about sponsoring our resolution?" You step off the moving staircase together, and separate. The day has begun.

January 25, 1958

I am spending a day and night with the Robertsons at our Embassy in Washington. Norman* seems stimulated here and is stimulating. This morning I had a ranging run over the possibilities of negotiations with the Russians with him and Ed Ritchie,† Norman seeing all sides but steering his purpose through his own subtleties. He said he has a few friends here — Dean Acheson, Walter Lippmann, and Frankfurter. He describes them as a sort of mandarin group *"not set* in their ideas but now become conservative or contemptuous, what proper mandarins should be," and then he adds, "Perhaps I am becoming 'set' myself." I can see no signs of it. Went to the National Gallery with Sylvia, and there among the Aztec death masks was Sammy Hood‡ — lounging, affectionate, welcoming — an El Greco in an old Etonian tie.

February 17, 1958

I loathe this official apartment in Sutton Place. There is no privacy, not a single door anywhere in the apartment, every room opens out onto another room, the furniture comes from Grand Rapids, the paintings are bad oil paintings by bad Canadian painters almost all in oranges and yellows of autumn colouring in the woods — a subject which should be put out of bounds for all Canadian artists. We have one maid, and by a curious stroke of fortune she is a German. Her salary is as much as that of the entire staff in Cologne, her name Matilda, her cooking inferior. Popski of course peed on the carpet on the day of his arrival. I can't say I care what he does to the carpet. It is a repulsive colour and covered with a sort of scurf that scuffs off on your shoes

*At this point Canadian Ambassador to Washington.

†A. E. Ritchie was to succeed me as Canadian Ambassador to the United States and was subsequently Under-Secretary of State for External Affairs.

‡Viscount Hood, then British Minister in Washington.

and gets all over your clothes. Every single time the
elevator goes up or down Popski barks.

March 5, 1958

I started the morning as I have most of the preceding
mornings — studying the Constitution and the Rules of
Procedure of the United Nations and, in particular, of the
Security Council, on which I am now the Canadian Repre-
sentative. We have before us the crisis over Tunisia, and
French actions there.

Lunched today with Bob Dixon, the British Representative. He seems very nice and intelligent with gentle
manners, almost a bedside manner. What do the British
make of one — "a sort of foreigner" who wears English
clothes and has an English accent, but is he *sound*?

The British Delegation are still recovering from the
wounds inflicted on them by the Suez crisis, when they
were virtually ostracized by friends and allies, not to
mention the enemies. Their line about Canada, and Mike
Pearson in particular, is one of appreciation and admiration for our role at that time, but I think these sentiments
come from the head and not the heart. In their hearts they
feel that their true friends were those like the Australians,
who backed them up to the hilt. It is from Moore Cros-
thwaite of their Delegation that I get a less guarded version
of their reactions. He is becoming a friend.

March 13, 1958

What an extraordinary coincidence it is that not only
is Matilda the cook German, but my secretary at the
Mission is of German origin, highly efficient and very
German in temperament. Went to one of the regular
meetings of the Commonwealth Representatives today.
Why is the British Representative always in the chair at
Commonwealth meetings? Would it not be much better

to rotate the chairmanship among the Commonwealth Representatives? Today Bob Dixon said to Arthur Lall, the Indian Representative, "I *think*, Arthur, that you will find mine is really quite an innocent little suggestion." "Too little and too innocent," said Lall, and I felt for him. Aly Khan is the news here. He has come as Representative of Pakistan. From elevator girls to sober-sided U.N. officials — they are all after him. Even when the men pretend to despise him as an amateur in international affairs, they want to get close to him so that they can tell their wives that this glamour boy is really only a balding little sallow-faced man. Bob Dixon's line is, "We should, I think, all do our very best to make him at home in the U.N. He is trying very hard." Exactly like a headmaster talking of a rich but erring boy who has come to his school with all registered intentions of "going straight". Arthur Lall is taking a line of extreme agreeableness, almost amounting to flirtatiousness, with the newcomer. Lall with all his pleasant manners gives off such a shine of malice from his highly polished surface and combines it with intellectual ability and an air of moral irreproachability. The fact that he has quite a good opinion of himself is the first, but perhaps not the last, impression left by him. Aly Khan's modesty and sense of humour are an attractive contrast.

March 16, 1958

As I write in the so-called den, Matilda moves maddeningly about in the sitting-room saying "Pfui" to Popski when he barks. Now she has begun Hoovering the carpet. She will end by driving me out into the street in a rage. There goes that infernal little beast barking again. Shall we ever escape from this flat-trap with its scurfy beige carpets, its dentist's-waiting-room furniture, its unopenable and unshuttable steel-framed windows? I am starting to look for a new apartment but the people in Ottawa are obstructing me at every turn.

March 17, 1958

St. Patrick's Day—a glorious day without a cloud. Went to meet Jules Léger* last night at the airport. The plane was two hours late and I sat happily alternating my reading between Descartes in a paper-bound edition and *Eloise in the Plaza*. In the afternoon to the Metropolitan Museum — the look of pride in the portraits of adventurers and dukes of Renaissance Italy, not vulgar assurances but the native vitality and splendour of men clothed in brilliant colours wearing strange hats, like birds of show and birds of prey with foreign markings, natives of another world. Where has that pride and splendour gone?

How much I like Jules. How wise and witty he is.

April 2, 1958

I had lunch with the Soviet Representative. He seems a homely old body, tough but not dehumanized. "We consider," he said, "that all religious wars have always been based entirely on economic motives. The name of religion merely masks the real motive, for example the Crusades." I said, "I cannot remember the economic motives for the Thirty Years War or the French religious wars, can you?" Apparently he could not. Brushing the question aside, he reverted to the Crusades.

In the afternoon we went to Mabel Ingalls's† farm in the country. She seemed in a nervous frenzy, jumping up from her chair to half open the window and then immediately shutting it again, smoking incessantly, quoting great names and then dashing them away again. Dorothy Osborne‡ sat with her long legs stretched out in dark-green woollen stockings and made her jerky, witty comments in her take-it-or-leave-it voice. Among the other

---

*Then Under-Secretary of State for External Affairs; subsequently Canadian Ambassador to France and Governor General of Canada.

†Daughter of J. P. Morgan, the banker.

‡Officer of the Department of External Affairs.

guests was a young couple who touched hands for a moment in physical recollection and could not help smiling at each other. Also a German count who could not — would not — believe that I was a Bad Shot. After lunch we threw things for the dogs to play with in front of the sitting-room fire. Rain streamed down in slanting slats across the flank of the mountain that Mabel has just bought to save it from the common herd and their motels, across her lake, her fields, her woods, her farms. We went home at 4 p.m. precisely. "What's your hurry?" growled Mabel.

April 18, 1958

Lunch with Engen, the Swedish Representative, and walked the sunny streets with him to his office. Banners hung from the tall buildings in the heat haze, vistas stretched, glass gleamed. Oh I love, absolutely love, New York, at any rate on a fine day in spring I do. Engen has a soft charm, a subtle intelligence, and a "progressive" outlook.

May 2, 1958

A feeling of respite today after my first day as President of the Security Council. Afterwards a journalist asked me what it was like being "up there in front of all the klieg lights with all the people watching. Can you give us the human angle or are you too hardened a diplomat?" The truth is that I very much enjoy the Security Council. It is rather like a court of law. When one is acting as the head of one's own delegation one is pleading a case, interjecting, cross-examining like a barrister. When one is in the chair one is interpreting the rules, keeping order, presiding like a judge. It is much less tiring than a diplomatic dinner party. The issue before the Security Council was the Soviet veto of the Northern Defence Zone. The Americans have prepared an International Arctic Inspection System and we have worked closely with them over this. Dag Hammarskjöld has supported it, much to the rage of the Russians. The "non-committed" countries were at first undecided as to the line they should take. What was decisive was the Soviet attitude, the blank lack of compromise, the Gromyko "nyet". We were back in the Cold War. Even if our tactics had been subtler, this would have changed nothing. During the disarmament negotiations this summer and even up to the last few weeks it has been possible to see some merit in the Russian case. This had its own consistency, but in this last week a new — or rather a return to an old — attitude has come about. Now they don't even bother to make a case. What does this change mean? A new access of strength from an unexpected quarter? Or the cover-up for a reappraisal? In the evening I had a television interview with Stan Burke. When the question-and-answer part of the interview was over they took what is called a reaction shot, during which he and I had to sit looking at each other for two interminable minutes before the camera. The more we gazed at each other eyeball to eyeball the more I felt a sensation of embarrassment which he perhaps shared.

May 9, 1958
Jetty* has been staying with us, looking young and pretty. When old Frederic Hudd† was boring her with the price of shad roe and his desire to acquire a brass-and-bronze platter with the head of Bacchus carved in relief upon it, she curled up on the sofa and went to sleep, looking like a young girl. As for old Frederic, he too looks younger now that the menopause is over. His face is thinner, his aquiline nose juts out like the nose on a death-mask although he is far from dead but pink and

*Jetty Robertson, wife of Norman A. Robertson.
†Formally senior official at Canada House, London.

perky, and in his relations with his host and hostess, Sir William* and Lady Stephenson, he makes me think of an undergraduate staying with two old people who "wait up for him" of an evening. After dinner he caused the lights to be turned out and recited the *Morte d'Arthur*, looking like a noble old Merlin himself. An actor he is — a ham actor. He is a Dickensian figure to me, one of those eccentrics whom the hero David Copperfield, or Pip, meets as a boy on his way upwards in life. I hope I am on Frederic's "prayer list", for although he says he is a phoney I should like his prayers. They might be potent all the same.

May 19, 1958

Oh this doorless flat, everyone's perpetual awareness of everyone else. It is like having no eyelids. At this moment Matilda is vacuuming the sitting-room (why at this hour?). If rays of hatred could strike her body through the archway that opens out from this parody of a library into the sitting-room, then dead at this instant would she fall. But who the hell do I think I am — Proust? — needing a cork-lined room to write a masterpiece when I am only scribbling this diary. Are my susceptibilities so exquisite? What would I do if my "dream children" were crying and shouting all around me? A crotchety old bore I am becoming. I have been reading *Justine* by Durrell. It depends on the mood — if you are irritated it will irritate you and you will say it is all shreds and patches of mysticism, aestheticism, and mandarinism. But wait — let the ingredients settle and the brew is seductive, disturbing, with strong, rancid flavours. Now as Popski barks I hear Matilda say in her plaintive high voice, "When he and I are alone together he is never like this, never barks. It is funny, very funny," and she gives a wild pipe of mirthless laughter.

*Sir William Stephenson was Director of British Security Co-ordination in the Western Hemisphere, 1940-6, and subject of *The Quiet Canadian*.

She is developing a mania for Popski and a sort of jealousy of us in competition for his love.

May 19, 1958

Mike Pearson and Maryon are here. He is taking part in a seminar on the TV—"In Search of an American Foreign Policy". He is in splendid form, entertaining and so intelligent, quite undismayed by political misfortunes. Maryon looking very handsome and being very funny and very much on the mark in her comments. I thought that the TV show itself was a dispiriting performance, conveying an impression of ineffectual uneasiness on the part of the Americans participating, with a note of sophomoric cynicism struck by the British Representative, Nutting.

May 24, 1958

These last days have been spent dabbling in this murky Lebanese crisis in the Security Council, where the Lebanese charge of interference in their internal affairs by Egypt is before the Council. Aksoul, the Lebanese Representative, comes to see me in the apartment at all hours for consultation, sometimes accompanied by his very decorative wife, who is herself no slouch in diplomatic negotiations. Last night when Aksoul was outlining the dangers facing the Lebanon, Popski came barking into the room and Aksoul said to me, "It is very nice to have a pet dog but is it so nice in such a small apartment?"—a question God knows I have often asked myself.

This Lebanese business is very tricky and one that could be dangerous, and as President of the Council I have to tread warily. Here my ignorance of the Middle East makes it difficult for me to gauge Arab reactions. I hate dealing with an area which I cannot see in my mind's eye and with people whose motives I cannot assess. Part of the difficulty is my ignorance of the history of that part of the world, which leaves me without terms of reference.

June 3, 1958

Our new Minister of External Affairs, Sidney Smith, has been here for a visit. He has been extremely kind and understanding in his dealings with me and I like him. He is shrewd enough too, but all the same I ask myself what can be the secret of his success. It is certainly not force of intelligence or grasp of issues. And he does talk such nonsense. Last night he began comparing Canada to his thirteen-year-old daughter, "both adolescents at the difficult age". He says, "We must not let ourselves be treated like Tunisians." What can he mean?

June 15, 1958

This Tunisian crisis, caused by the French bombing of a Tunisian border village, has exercised my mind and my feelings too without respite for days. I live in the U.N. like a termite in cheese and my personal life has disappeared. I stay on and on in the evening in the office until I suppose the staff say, "He works because he has nothing else in his life."

What is disturbing is the resentment which has grown up between us and the British over the Middle East — echoes of Suez involved. I should like to be in agreement with them, even — if necessary — against the United States. That used to be the state of affairs. For example, over Korea we worked well together. I wish I could talk to some Englishman freely and have it all out — perhaps Harold Beeley or Humphrey Trevelyan, * not Bob Dixon. He would just pretend to agree with me. What worries me is what worried me at the time of Suez and was not a moral question but a sharp divergence as to the possibilities. They seem to me to be suffering from an aberration and in pursuit of it to be oblivious of their loss of reputation.

*Sir Harold Beeley, then Deputy U. K. Representative to the U.N., later Ambassador to Egypt; Sir Humphrey Trevelyan, formerly British Ambassador to Egypt, then Under-Secretary at the U.N., now Lord Trevelyan.

They proceed by indirection, pretend to scruples, perhaps even feel them, but they do not count the full cost in the Middle East or clearly see the end in view.

June 21, 1958

Last night I went, at his invitation, to call on President Heuss (President of the German Federal Republic) whom I had known when I was posted in Bonn. The moment I got into the hotel sitting-room I was transported back to the peculiar atmosphere of all such German gatherings. There was a real wish on their part to make a graceful gesture to a former Canadian Ambassador to their country. There was even genuine friendliness, and the old man himself was as charming and natural as ever, yet still the occasion had a sort of stuffiness and clumsiness like so many German official gatherings. This was mainly produced by the gang of officials surrounding the President. What do I feel when I look back on the Germans and my relations with them? I feel a sort of twisted liking for them and admiration too, but their lack of ease is painful, as is their incessant struggle to impose themselves and an undercurrent of doubt as to whether they are succeeding, the incessant grinding of their *will* to stamp a rigid form on their self-consciousness, to button up their nature.

June 26, 1958 — Ottawa, on a visit for consultation

I am off for a walk around the poop-deck of Parliament Hill which overlooks the river where I have so often walked in the past trying to regain balance after some crisis in my Ottawa life. When I see the tired, aging men who are my friends and who work in the Department I think it is as well that I don't have to face that ordeal. There is something wrong here but it is the same thing that it has always been — overwork, the panic desire to escape before they get too old, and the fascination of being in the centre of things, these pulling in opposite directions. I know that dilemma and I have no desire to go through it all over again.

July 2, 1958 — New York in a heat wave

I am alone in the flat. Sylvia has stayed on in Ottawa. Matilda and Popski are away on a holiday. I sleep in one bed and then in another and I never make up the one I slept in last. I leave my dirty clothes in piles on the floor. If the light doesn't work, I'm too lazy to change the bulb, so just move to another room. Elizabeth writes that Bowen's Court is becoming for her a barrack of anxiety and that she has to face the fact that she cannot keep it up any longer and must sell it. She writes, "I am getting bored here and that is a fact. I suppose it is the effect of hardening my heart. When one can no longer afford to support an illusion one rather welcomes seeing it break down, or perhaps, in this case, run down," but does she really know how much leaving Bowen's Court will hurt when the time comes?

Had dinner last night with an old friend from Nova Scotia, now a very successful New York career woman. It was interesting to see how the acquired layers of New York "graciousness and culture" came peeling off after the third drink. Thank God they did.

October 16, 1958

I spent the morning trying to work on the Minister's (Sidney Smith) speech on disarmament to be delivered to the General Assembly. The truth of the matter is that I am discouraged as I have been working on disarmament now off and on for months and I can see no prospect of achieving anything substantial. The same unreality hangs over so many of the activities of this year's General Assembly — the abolition of apartheid, the bill on international human rights, peace in the Middle East, peace in the Far East, disarmament. Who thinks we can achieve any of these things? It is likely to be easier to get to the moon. Anyway, diplomats are only small craftsmen and there are no statesmen.

John Holmes came to lunch today. He is here with the Delegation as special adviser. John is probably one of the most liked diplomats in the United Nations, a real asset to Canada. He should be in this job instead of me. He gets on easy terms with all, the more exotic the better. Indo-Chinese princes, Polish communists, Indian intellectuals — all eat out of his hand.

Well, I must get on with that speech. I can't leave all the work to John just because I am suffering from "cosmic disillusionment". He has been through all that himself and come out a patient, modest Christian (although not Christian by faith he certainly is by temperament).

For my part, I lost my temper in a most un-Christian way with Krishna Menon, who is heading the Indian Delegation to the General Assembly, yesterday. It does not seem by his attitude today to have done any harm at all to our relations, rather the reverse. The odd part is that I have a grudging, suspicious admiration for the creature. I can't help seeing that he has political imagination and a kind of wild, malicious high spirits. When he comes into the Commonwealth delegation meetings he flutters the dovecotes just for the fun of it. Poor old Alan Noble, the head of the British Delegation, who is chairman of the committee, is like an ineffectual schoolmaster trying to keep a brilliant bad boy under control. Just how bad is Krishna Menon? Perhaps worse than we think.

October 20, 1958

I spent all last evening with Sidney Smith and John going over the speech until I got quite bleary-eyed and was also suffering from indigestion caused by bad curry. Sid has a dual personality. First there is the over-confident, wordy, artful one — and then, over his shoulder, there is a perceptive, sensitive Sid who appears to judge his companion harshly although he always gives way to him. This is an unkind way to write of him. He has been exceptionally friendly and nice to me. He wasn't too bad working on the speech, either. When he gets hold of a point of policy he sticks to it, and he changed the tone for the better and some of the individual phrases. The text we were working on for this speech was John's and I dare say he must have felt a bit bruised as his text was being mauled and battered about, but he is so patient and objective that he gave no sign of irritation, as I certainly would have done.

It is still before breakfast and the red sun has just risen over the river. I have been standing on the balcony looking down to where it broadens towards Brooklyn Bridge and beyond to the sea. I love that widening of the river. I don't know how I shall live without it when we change apartments.

November 5, 1958

As I was walking along 34th Street near Pennsylvania Station while waiting for my train to the country (it was a brilliantly fine morning), a certain gentleman caught up with me and, walking a few blocks together, we joined in conversation. "New York," he said, "is a murderous city. You have to know what you can do here and what you can't or you get yourself a bad ulcer. That is why I walk every morning for an hour before I go to my business." He was the manager of Coward's Shoe Store, a wise man sent from God, for as he talked, glancing at me from under his battered hat with sharp, dark eyes, I felt my own tension relax and I walked happily among the skyscrapers, the slum door stoops, the cheap restaurants, and the building sites down by the river under a blue heaven.

November 7, 1958

I wrote off in answer to that nice little German Gräfin's letter about Aga Fürstenburg's death. Mine was an empty, careful letter. She must have known that Aga and I were friends. Poor Aga, "warm-hearted, courageous, witty" I wrote of her. But that is not the point. Unhappy, near-desperate, turning herself and everything else into a joke, with her "grande dame" manner and her wild gossip. She remained hopelessly attached to her Prussian baron but I think she was not lucky in love or money. She had no reason to live and did not like it much, but she was much more alive than those who have reasons for living and do like it.

November 16, 1958

Weekend with the Angels at their farm in Connecticut. A Sunday-morning walk under the grey sky through a country of small fields enclosed in grey stone walls, and back to drink bourbon out of Victorian moustache cups (Mr. Angel collects them), in company with a group of pleasant late-middle-aged couples. This is a converted farmhouse, full of charm. The Angels and their friends have lots and lots of money, but never too much in evidence. They're people who have travelled, collected good furniture, shot big game, farmed the land, run businesses or law firms, "kept up" with art, literature, and politics. Most have been married several times. (The interests they have, these Americans! The information they have modestly and unemphatically accumulated while also accumulating so much else.)

December 15, 1958

At last the General Assembly is over and yesterday the Canadian Delegation got off by plane for Ottawa. The weeks of pressure all day and late into the night are over, and the effort of keeping so many balls in the air. I have tried to run a private social life on the margin of the great circus of the General Assembly. I have even succeeded in doing so, at the moderate cost of a ruined digestion.

December 20, 1958

On the Ocean Limited between Moncton and Amherst on my way to Halifax for Christmas leave, during an interminable wait. Why is the train waiting? Frozen up, I suppose, in the midst of this waste of snow and scrubby fir trees. It is darkening quickly outside the train windows and is getting cold inside this compartment. Probably the heating goes off when the train is not in motion. There! she gave a jolt. Does that mean that we are going to move? No, not an inch, and we'll be four hours late arriving.

Yesterday, sitting alone in the long gallery of the Windsor Hotel in Montreal, I opened my eyes on the dark panelling and the windows inset with armorial glass and the large, obscure paintings in their immense frames. The gallery was half-lit and silent, with snow coming down the well shaft beyond the sightless glazed windows. The housekeeper came along and switched on a table lamp. "A little light might help," she said; "such a beautiful room, and it's all to be demolished next year. They will never replace a ceiling like that."

I determined to take a taxi and go out to Saint Anne de Bellevue to see my cousin Gerald. There he was in a corner of the ward among all the other ex-servicemen of the First War. He has been moved now from the mental ward. He looked tiny, shrivelled and shrunk, plucked-looking, with huge blue eyes in his ageless face. He sat up straight in his wheelchair with his destroyed hands in his lap. Round his shoulders was a scarlet shawl. We forced conversation with each other across his bed-table about the Queen, Russia, his pills. "Things," he said, "are not too bad with me, and not too good." I talked to his nurse by the door. She praised his courage in standing pain; never a groan or a movement of impatience. Is there something uncanny about him, I thought, as he watched us talking with an ironic expression; a sort of saint has he become? I thought of him writing a card to my mother in the depths of his melancholy madness, "Nil desperandum", and I thought if he could say that, shall I always be able to?

February 5, 1959 — New York

It *is* the most uncanny thing that whenever I try to write or read, Matilda the German maid appears and begins to tidy, to water the plants right under my nose, to turn down the bedspreads, to empty the ashtrays. The moment the woman sees one settling down to work she comes in to fuss like a bluebottle. We are back in our high-up twenty-first-floor apartment, with the wind beating off the East River. High up as it is, it did not prevent our being robbed the night before last. Yes, a burglar came into this very bedroom between three and four in the morning and stole from the drawer by my bed what money there was, which unluckily was too much. It is strange to know that he, or she, was probing about in the dark while we stupidly, blindly, slept and the burglar coolly got away with the money from the sleeping suckers. Being robbed makes one feel such a damn fool.

February 21, 1959

I am doing an assessment of the personality of Cabot Lodge, who is spoken of as a possible Secretary of State to succeed Foster Dulles. I have struck up a real friendship with Cabot, unlikely as it seems, as no two people could be more different. He is full of courage and energy, extremely impatient, and permanently at odds with Dulles. I think any American Representative at the U.N. will always end up on bad terms with the State Department. Living and operating in the atmosphere of the United Nations inevitably changes one's point of view. There are tactical advantages to be gained here. There is the temptation of publicity and popularity, not appreciated by Foreign Offices at home, and this is particularly true of the New York/ Washington axis. Cabot's weakness is his emotionalism, which would indeed be a fatal weakness in a Secretary of State who had to negotiate with the Russians. I am never sure whether this emotionalism is genuine or whether it is a stunt for public consumption.

I find him very good company. When Mrs. Roosevelt was here with the American Delegation and I was sitting beside her at dinner, I said to her, "I am very fond of Cabot," and she drew back her lips over her teeth and said, "How very interesting. You are the first person I have ever met who was *fond* of Cabot Lodge."

February 22, 1959

Old John Stevenson, who was for so many years the London *Times* correspondent in Ottawa, came in for a drink. I like him, but he is full of scurrilous and inaccurate stories. Strangely enough, as he has got older he has almost stopped being a bore and seems to have returned to an earlier self — more considerate, more affectionate, less apt to hog the conversation. I have noticed that onset of mildness and moderation in aging old egotists before now. It is perhaps a sign that their end is not far off.

Talking of bores, I made a speech to the Bullock Forum about the United Nations yesterday which bored me almost as much as it must have bored the audience. In return they gave me a silver replica of Nelson's dress sword in the form of a paper-opener.

In the afternoon to a cocktail party at Mary McCarthy's. Elizabeth Bowen says Mary would say anything about a friend, but do anything to help him, or her.

March 8, 1959

I sit here trying to write. Matilda, her hair in curl-papers, comes tidying things under my nose. Then she begins to shake two bathroom mats out of the window on to the terrace. Then she changes the cigarette in my ashtray beside my notebook so that all the smoke goes into my eyes. She has a passion for Popski. She takes him away for weekends with her to stay with her German sister — puts him in a box with an air-hole in it. He seems to accept this with resignation, although he has bitten her three times.

I am reading a book about the American Revolution. As I was brought up in a nest of United Empire Loyalists, I always instinctively sympathize with them, but I am swinging to the side of the Revolution. How insufferable it must have been for the Americans to be patronized by petty British officials and third-rate line officers.

What am I to do about these damn diaries? I know what I *should* do — destroy them. Perhaps the bank will be bombed with them in it, perhaps I shall lose them. I don't want to leave them as a mess behind me, which might cause pain or hurt people's feelings. It is very odd how little mention there is in them of my working life.

Talking about work, I have done about five drafts of a long paper on Germany, German rearmament, the possibilities of reunification, Canadian policy towards Germany, and I was pleased to hear that my piece is to be used by the Prime Minister as the basic paper on the subject for his talks with Harold Macmillan.

March 23, 1959

Dag Hammarskjöld lunched here the other day to meet Elizabeth Bowen, who is here on a visit. They both set out to please each other and succeeded. He does not relax easily in the company of women and most women do not take kindly to him. The sexual element is missing and he cannot be bothered replacing it by cozy persiflage. Women sense a certain chill. Elizabeth, I thought, would not be drawn to him — a neuter Swede could not be attrac-

tive to her. As it turned out, she was at first surprised, then
charmed and amused. With his customary quickness he
caught on at once to the fact that this was no sentimental
lady novelist but a mind as capable as his own of dealing in
general ideas. From this understanding there was only a
jump to pleasure in each other's company. He left behind
him the mountaineer idealist and sparked with witty,
clever sketches of people and places, absurd situations, and
indiscreet imitations of public personalities — a side of him
that he too seldom shows and perhaps deliberately keeps
under surveillance. This was for him a day out of school.
When Elizabeth exercises her charm it can attract anyone
from the charwoman to the Duke of Windsor, with whom
she got on so well that evening in Paris. She is desperately
worried about money and says she is more and more
irritated by what she calls the Fortnum and Mason troubles
of the rich, such as the cost of double-silk linings for
drawing-room curtains.

June 1, 1959

Alastair Buchan* is here today and we have been
sitting drinking gins and tonics on the terrace. He has just
come back from Ottawa and says that the atmosphere there
is very claustrophobic. This is partly due to the Diefenbaker régime and the bad relations between the government and the civil service resulting from the suspicion of
Ministers, and particularly the Prime Minister, that the
higher civil servants may be disloyal to the government, or
even plotting with the Liberals against them. In a way this
suspicion is comprehensible. In the long years in Opposition the Conservative Members of Parliament, particularly
the Western Members of Parliament, have been living a
somewhat isolated life in their rented houses and apart-

---

*Hon. Alastair Buchan, journalist and author, and the son of John
Buchan, Lord Tweedsmuir. He was Director of the Institute of Strategic
Studies.

ments in Ottawa. They have seen the cozy, intimate relationship between Liberal Ministers and civil servants, mostly living cheek-by-jowl in Rockcliffe, their children attending the same schools, their wives in and out of each other's houses, intimate old friendships between senior civil servants and Ministers, and so they have come to believe in a sort of conspiracy against the government. It is true, I imagine, that most of the influential civil servants in Ottawa have Liberal sympathies, certainly very few are Conservatives, but I think they are much too loyal to the tradition of an impartial civil service to work against the government. Unfortunately, this intense suspicion of their motives and behaviour may create the very animosity that it fears.

June 8 to June 13, 1959 — Ottawa

I arrived on a hot, thunderous evening and drove straight to the Country Club for dinner to meet the new Minister of External Affairs, Howard Green. The taxi-driver said that in this weather he had to change his shirt twice a day because it stuck with sweat to the back of the car seat. At the Country Club the senior members of the Department were standing about in a rather stilted, uneasy way waiting to meet the "new boss". I could hear Norman Robertson's* host laugh coming through the windows into the Club, where I was hastily pouring myself a preliminary drink. As it turned out, the dinner went surprisingly well and the Minister made a very good start with us. He was skilful and tactful, with an ironic sense of humour. What kind of impression the members of the Department made on him it is harder to say.

In the afternoon I went to see my brother Roley's swearing-in as a judge of the Supreme Court. Nothing has

*Norman A. Robertson had returned from Washington and was now Under-Secretary of State for External Affairs.

ever given me more deep satisfaction than his now being what his nature, ability, and heredity meant him to be.

June 28, 1959

Marshal Berland came to lunch with me today. He talked of Elizabeth. He loves and reveres her for her goodness, intelligence, and generosity of heart. So, twenty years later, she is still able to mould, to inspire, and to amuse another young nature. I told him that even when she was gone, and however long he lived, her quickening influence would still work on his imagination. He seemed today to me to be like myself when young — a mixture of romanticism, quick sympathy, and quick cynicism.

We dined with the Japanese Ambassador, my new friend Matsudiara. He is quite unlike any other Japanese I have met. He is worldly and witty, and is extremely indiscreet. He plays the Japanese hand cleverly at the U.N. but is not, I think, quite at ease with the Afro-Asian group of nations, of which Japan is of course a member. Indeed, there does not seem to be much natural sympathy between the Japanese and the Africans. The Afro-Asians as a group are proving increasingly difficult to deal with. Either in bilateral negotiations or with the Commonwealth members in a Commonwealth framework, relations are easier, but as a group the Afro-Asians are showing an increasing tendency to take up extreme positions and to produce resolutions full of sound and fury and quite inoperable. This, of course, is not only true of Afro-Asians.

Another new friend — or one who could become a friend — of a very different kind is the poet Howard Moss, whom I met through Elizabeth. How funny and perceptive he is, charming, and with a fibre of integrity.

We are beginning to make the move from this apartment in Sutton Place to the new one in Park Avenue. Matilda does not go with us. Meanwhile, she has bought a new *toupet* which makes her look like a housekeeper in a detective play.

August 15, 1959 — Stonington, Connecticut

I have the precarious feeling that I shall be interrupted at any moment as I am sitting up here in the cool
top room of this pretty little house, or simply that I shall
get too sleepy because it is so hot and still outside in the
garden and so silent in the house, except for the faint
clinking of dishes being washed in the distant kitchen.
The noise of insects strumming tunelessly, or according to
their own tunes, fills the air. There are three or four other
people staying in the house. "What it must be in this heat
in New York!" everyone says. This is a woman's house —
wallpapers "enchantingly gay", the house painted pink
outside, a former farmhouse but it has left the manure pile
far, far behind. There is a garden, or rather an enclosed
lawn, shaded by immense maples (or are they ash? I must
look) and walled with a stone wall about the height of a
man. I know I bored my hostess, Mary, last night. She
looked quite effaced with boredom, her face like one in a
murky mirror. She is a delightful creature, with mind,
feeling, and wit.

August 16, 1959 — Stonington

Hotter still today, although a faint breeze is moving
in the branches of the tree outside the window. Prideaux,
the drama critic of *Time* magazine, has joined the house
party. He is a cozy character but could bite if he chose.

Stonington is a charming little town, eighteenth-
century white clapboard houses with fanlights over the
doors. In one Mrs. Carlton Sprague-Smith practises
chamber music and collects white Wedgwood stone china.
In another Miss Bull perfects fine book-binding in a pre-
Revolutionary hide-out in her herb garden. We dine on
terraces here and there with these acquaintances and they
in turn come for drinks in the garden, but tonight it is too
thundery for the garden. Perhaps if I went downstairs I
might get a drink, although it is really too early for one

and it would not do for me to help myself from our hostess's whisky when she is not about.

August 22, 1959 — New York

We are in the final stages of moving from the flat. We camp in the sitting-room with garden furniture. Nothing is left in this place but beds, TV, and tooth-brushes, and the incessant wind blowing from the air-conditioner. Sylvia has been working packing things all day for the last two days, while I have been sitting reading. Last night she asked me would I move the window-box from the ledge on the terrace. I went out, picked it up, but it was heavier than I thought and I dropped it on the front of my foot, breaking two small bones. Serves me right for being so lazy. The chauffeur took me to Saint Luke's Hospital to have a cast put on which will be with me for a month. Sylvia says it is the last time she will ask me to help with moving anything.

September 22, 1959

We are installed in the new flat. It is much larger and rented principally for entertainment during the General Assembly. The Supplies and Properties Division of the Department of External Affairs has spent a good deal on doing it up but for some mysterious reason they refuse to renew the wooden seat on the W.C. of the spare room. I pointed out to them that prongs of wood had come loose from the seat and were sticking out, to the danger of anyone sitting on it. Still they refused. Finally, today, I telephoned them and said that as the Minister was coming to stay it would be their responsibility if any of these wooden prongs stuck into the ministerial bottom. They gave way at once and I have now authority for a new W.C. seat. Truly, the Department of External Affairs works in mysterious ways.

September 27, 1959

Howard Green, the new Minister of External Affairs, has arrived for the General Assembly and we have started, he and I, by having a falling-out. I am upset about this as I feel a rapidly increasing admiration and affection for him, but at the Delegation meeting this morning he publicly rejected my advice. It has to do with the French action in Tunisia, and my pro-French predilection got the upper hand of me. I must say that my support for French positions seems a one-sided effort, as the French never make the slightest attempt to accommodate us. Does he think that as an official of the suspect Department of External Affairs I am working against him in some way? On the policy question he may be quite right and I quite wrong. In fact, he probably is right.

October 1, 1959

All is well again between me and the Minister. He is very impressive in dealing with other delegations but I am sometimes rather alarmed by his technique and the way in which he sweeps aside arguments and opposition. However, he does not seem in the least alarmed. He certainly gave Bob Dixon the surprise of his life yesterday. I couldn't help laughing in my bath this morning when I thought about it. Bob, as chairman of the Commonwealth meeting, made a statement on policy at the Assembly which he hoped would be acceptable to us. He produced these views with quiet, persuasive confidence and was about to pass on to another item on the agenda when the Minister said, "In our best judgement, that simply doesn't make sense." I think there will be quite a lot of broken crockery left about when the Minister returns to Ottawa and I can see that I am going to have to pick up a lot of the pieces. Those who think that they have got a nice tame Canadian in the new Minister are very much mistaken. He is a very shrewd politician. He is also admirable in his pursuit of objectives in which he tenaciously believes, particularly in the field of disarmament.

October 2, 1959

Strauss, the German Defence Minister, came today for talks with the Minister, accompanied by the German Ambassador to Ottawa, Dankwort, and a group of German officials. While Strauss was talking to the Minister, Dankwort kept whispering to me about nothing in a low voice, thus reminding me of that irritating trick of German officials. When their superiors are present they always talk in a low, reverent murmur as if they were in church. Strauss put on a performance of jovial, shrewd frankness which was very nearly convincing. Despite his grossness he can be attractive. The Minister, who has not seen a German since he killed some of them in the First World War, was fascinated by the interestingness of Strauss's talk, his disregard for platitude, his realism and no-nonsense approach.

January 15, 1960

Outside the door the official Cadillac awaits and I begin to think of what is to be done today. In the office my secretary (except when she suffers from a delaying migraine) waits, gently and satirically. She reminds me of my oversights with a tiny pinprick. The incoming telegrams are piled before me, the news of the world extrapolated for my benefit. These chalk-blue messages and white replies contain a scenario of the World's Game. They inform and they disguise. A riot or a revolution comes to one without the movement of fear or rage, couched in the cool telegraphese of our Chargés d'Affaires. Policy is indicated in faint loop-like shapes. It is to be flexibly firm and firmly flexible. Aims fade into a Technicolor sunset of world peace, the Declaration on Human Rights excludes the nightmare and sounds like an invitation to a plate lunch at the Waldorf. Disarmament is to be complete, but hate they cannot regulate. This paper world breeds paper conflicts in the mind, starchy debates between the one hand and the other, and peering to descry the barricades on which we ought to die. It is no go, all that; it is none of our business anyway, for we are diplomats, not meant to think or feel but to manipulate and remember and to shift the papers from the "In" box to the "Out".

Then there is the little matter of personal relations with other governments and, most important, with one's own. How to put things — in a way — you know — in a certain fashion which does not offend and yet disturbs. How to hide the needle in the bundle of hay.

Of course, Canadians are different. There is no malice in us. We are the family doctor whom no one has called in for consultation. We are the children of the midday who see all in the clear, shallow light.

January 16, 1960

Certainly one does not at any particular time of life from day to day feel the same age. On one day one may feel a premonition of what it will be like to be really old, and on another one awakes again an adolescent. Quivers of restlessness, flushes of vanity, tail-ends of impossible dreams disturb. One even craves the moral anarchy — like a lost innocence — of adolescence. Oh for the breakdown of Values, those weights upon the lids of life!

The Argentine Ambassador says that the access of sensuality in middle-aged men is called in his country "le démon du midi", after a forgotten novel on this subject by

Paul Bourget. He says that the title refers to a phrase in the Psalms, which I must look up.

I telephoned my mother today in Halifax. I don't know how to deal with her old age. Perhaps when I am with her, by refusing to admit it I seem to make light of an unbearable affliction. My pretence that she is as she always was may be superficially flattering but may seem like silly patronage (who does he think he is taking in?), and am I not forcing her to play up to my pretence? Is that love? In love all barriers are down, and she has always tried to pull them down to show me the truth. She is indeed preoccupied with the business of dying and sends courageous and despairing signals as she is drawn away on an irresistible tide, and yet they say to me, "How amusing your mother was yesterday! Isn't she wonderful!"

January 24, 1960

I wonder if I can write at all without echoing the truly terrible style in which this book *Advise and Consent* is written. Norman Robertson says that it is "a good political novel". For him and for me it comes pat on the occasion. This is what we are up against in Ottawa — the jungle of politics. Of course, we have always been up against it, but for some illusory years we seemed cushioned against its savageries; in the jungle of politics when the powerful beast strikes one can hide or run, melt into protective colouring if any can be found — but don't wander unarmed in the deceptive sunshine of the glades or you may get badly bruised, finally mauled. I have just been talking to such a victim of power politics. He will live, but will he ever fully recover?

I had lunch today with David Walker.* He has just finished a new book. He said that as he was getting

*Canadian novelist.

towards the end of it he developed a fear that he might die before he had time to finish it and hardly liked to go near the tractor on his farm in case he met with a fatal accident. When David told me this I had a flash of the deepest, most hopeless envy. What would I not give to feel myself the carrier of a book in which I believed!

January 28, 1960

I am a little worried by my speech yesterday. Huntingdon Gilchrist said I had given people something to think about. I felt that this was just what I had not done.

With luck — I mean, if nothing goes wrong, illness, scandal, disfavour of the great, or conspicuous failure — I may expect to stay on at the United Nations for two or even three years. Then there is a possibility of the Under-Secretaryship in Ottawa. But it may be that they would prefer to offer it to someone younger, and perhaps they would do better to do so. Then there is the possibility that Washington may become vacant and they may want a useful, non-controversial successor and I might be the one. Or there is Delhi soon to be vacant — and to be resisted at all costs. Two or three more postings and it is all over. Then retirement and we call it a day.

Harold Beeley of the British Delegation, whom I think of as an educated man, told me that he could never read philosophy and could not understand a word of it. This made me feel better about my struggles with Stuart Hampshire's book. * But it does all the same seem idiotic that two grown men like him and me, who are reputedly intelligent at their jobs and who have had expensive educations, are apparently incapable of following a discussion on questions of mind conducted in what looks — deceptively — like plain English.

*Stuart Hampshire, the British philosopher, had published *Thought in Action* in 1959.

February 9, 1960

I think and hope that Canada is respected in the United Nations. Or is it just that we are regarded as "respectable"? We seem to have assumed the role in many of the world's troubles as an objective bystander, willing to help if it does not cost too much, given to tut-tutting over the passionate unreasonableness of other people, and quite given to political moralizing. It seems to me that we Canadians have been lucky enough so far to ourselves be spared any "moment of truth". I think there is altogether too much glossing over of the real issues in our statements on defence and foreign policy, both by the Government and by the Opposition. There is also a dated "progressive" political vocabulary which is supposed to give a mildly advanced look to our policies but which is often very superficial and could be misleading.

February 21, 1960

I spent the morning with Hammarskjöld, who was in marvellous form, giving me vignettes of the political leaders with whom he has been dealing — Salazar, de Gaulle, and Franco. He is certainly the most charming, witty, intelligent companion and a delight to be with, glinting with malice and playing with political schemes, ideas, devices, and stratagems.

March 9, 1960

March is perhaps the most unpleasant month in the year. Dirty snow in the streets and the cracking and raking of a snow shovel on the pavement, raw sunlight, hard blue sky, and a back-breaking wind.

For some reason I woke up today thinking of Anne. I seemed to see her at the front door of Lapford as her brother Tony and I drove up the avenue in his battered second-hand car, coming from Oxford, where we had begun to be friends. There she stands, her dark head consciously averted, flanked by her mother and her two Chekov aunts. Lapford Grange was enclosed in a green Devon combe. The house was comfortable, rather shabby — not that one noticed — and full of people. I see a young girl, a Romantic Young Girl, with a strongly developed feeling of herself as a Romantic Young Girl, yet with a streak of realism, no silliness, she delights precipitately in her cleverness, she is avid for life, grasping for it. She is sensuous, sentimental, easily in tears or laughter, deliciously eager.

Yes, I remember her, looking like a Russian girl in one of the novels she loved, with her untidy dark hair, her mesmeric dark eyes, her fine-wristed hands. How she talked, with what urgency!

Then I began thinking of Oxford and, inevitably, of Billy Coster, that meteor of my skies till he blunted his wits with drink and became an embarrassing bore. He belonged to the Scott Fitzgerald age and was like Diver in *Tender Is the Night*; like him in his social fascination and his underlying truculence. He was a sexual nihilist, not to be confused with a neuter. He spoke and seemed like an Englishman and I thought of him as the only American who was not like an American. I think now that his was a very American tragedy. In his last phase during the War he lived almost entirely with dart-playing London pals whom he had picked up at his fire-watching station, and sought solace in a semi-platonic friendship with a good-natured barmaid. He thought the English lower classes better friends than his own class and he romanticized them. He would drink beer, port, and whisky all in one hour. He tried to escape from America, from money, and from sex, and died in his mother's arms in an alcoholic clinic in California. I loved Billy and laughed with him and drank with him and talked with him for hours on end. Later, we were both at Harvard as post-graduates and hated Cambridge together. If he appeared today as he first was, how life would come to life. How truly awful it would be if he appeared again as he ended. Dear Billy, how he would have hated the United Nations. He loathed cant. He also thought he loathed snobbery, but he was a New York gentleman and in his heart believed it hard to beat the Costers and the Schermerhorns. No one seems to remember him now — not even his relations. Perhaps he was an embarrassment from which they are delivered. His mother is dead, too — fascinating, funny, with her handsome face and wild stylishness. I see her in trailing tea-gowns, in the sitting-room of some hotel suite in London, Paris, or New York, upbraiding, mocking, and moaning over her children and applying her own disastrous touch to their general débâcle. And where has all the money gone? To "little Matilda", I suppose, the child of the Paris Ritz, married to a duke — must be nearly forty by now. I might sit next to her at dinner without recognizing her. But Billy is Down Among the Dead Men. If he is in Paradise, it is the Oxford of his youth, where he shone briefly in the warmth of friendship and the sparkle of high spirits.

We were all "children of the twenties". But is that phrase just an escape-hatch to excuse messy, self-indulgent, frivolous lives? Is it like blaming alcoholism on heredity, or crime on "something that happened in one's childhood"? In fact, is there anything in this twenties business? Not much perhaps, but something. The famous frivolity marked us, as did the fashionable despair. We also were "rebels without a cause".

April 13, 1960

On this fine spring morning with the sun and the cool breeze and New York traffic sounds coming up from the street I feel hungry and cheerful. Elizabeth is up the Hudson at Poughkeepsie, having taken on a seminar at Vassar. She says the whole place is threaded with stories, a frieze of young creatures drifting across the campus, the girls going to collect their letters like going to collect eggs on the farm, and the girl coming back reading a letter as she walks and smiling to herself. Elizabeth says hang on to the diaries — they could be pruned and published as "The Diaries of Mr. X".

May 14, 1960
A large, cheerful lunch party today at the Piping Rock Club in Locust Valley. More and more rich Americans, and how endlessly many there seem to be and how endlessly much money they seem to have — and when you think of all the other rich Americans who don't happen to be meeting one at lunch or dinner in the month of May 1960, the thought becomes quite oppressive. Then there is this talk of private planes and swimming-pools and "We have taken a floor at the Plaza for six months", "Her mother has inherited the most divine villa at Como", "He has the largest collection of Fabergé in the world", "They own two miles of private beach on the Sound", "Our plantation near Charleston" — and what is nice is that they are all rich together. Ambassadors, too, are collected for social occasions — the house-trained ones.

August 15, 1960
Just back from my holiday in Nova Scotia. The Minister has arrived by plane from Ottawa. Went back to the hotel with him from the airport. Of course, in spite of my instructions, no one from the Delegation had inspected their rooms. The heat was appalling and there was no air-conditioner in their sitting-room. Naturally, my flowers for Mrs. Green had not been delivered. Then there was a meeting over his disarmament speech. Tommy Stone, Wally Nesbitt, Ross Campbell, Geoff Murray, and myself — what a lot of high-priced help! The speech was immensely long but I think very well reasoned.

August 20, 1960

The first morning that I can breathe again after five days of the Minister's presence in New York, during which he brought off a very neat little ploy on disarmament, sent up his prestige, and got what he wanted by a mixture of toughness and shrewdness that surprised and impressed his fellow professional politician, Cabot Lodge, while at the same time stealing the show from him. I think Cabot may have thought that he was dealing with a nice old boy from the sticks who was a little slow in the uptake and could be patronized with his usual effortless effrontery — but it did not work out like that. This exercise demonstrated the advantage of taking an inflexible and clear-cut position at the start, in our case a middle position towards which the "uncommitted" countries in the U.N. gyrated. During this time I was somewhat irritated by Mark, who came down with the Canadian Delegation. He has all the virtues but occasionally relies too much on possessing them. He "cannot tell a lie", when no one actually is asking him to do so, so why the protuberant stare of aggressive integrity? Someone said of him, "He is a stallion." Yes, but a stallion with a conscience.

August 22, 1960

"When will this weather change?" the doorman asked as I stepped out from under the apartment-house awning into the heat of 62nd Street. These hot, sticky days seem to have been with us for so long that we have lost track of dates and can hardly remember when they began or what went before them. The cool sparkle of early autumn seems a distant mirage. Central Park is not really any cooler than the streets but I go there every morning to walk over the burnt grass and under the dusty trees before we have breakfast in the apartment. I get my first cup of coffee in the Zoo cafeteria and take it out on to the terrace.

The coffee tastes of dishwater, the terrace tables have not yet been cleaned, and when I put my elbow on the green-painted table surface, grains of sugar stick to the sleeve of my coat. At a nearby table Zoo attendants in open-necked khaki shirts are gossiping about the animals. Sometimes I overhear something that interests me — the cause of the squabble between the gorilla and his mate, the reason why the lioness lies moaning on her back with her paws in the air. The animals are still half asleep at this hour, but they have already come or been pushed out into their outdoor cages. They seem cross or reluctant to begin their day. Only the seals are enjoying themselves, the sole cool creatures in New York, gliding and snorting in the dirty water of their pool.

Inside the apartment, breakfast is waiting on the small table between the windows in Sylvia's bedroom, the *New York Times* beside one chair, the *Herald Tribune* beside the other. Popski is lying on the unmade bed, his head burrowing under the sheets, his rump immobile. Anne, the new maid, brings in more coffee. Her morning face is like her evening one — round, porcelain pink and white. She must have been a pretty girl, plump probably even then.

Outside the windows is the racket of the electric drill as they burrow away at the destruction of the apartment-house next door. You can see down into rooms like our own, minus their ceilings. Sylvia is a thorough newspaper reader. She questions what the Medical Association say in their statement. I read the foreign political news and about animals and architecture. After the egg comes a cigarette. Shaving, thank God, is over, the face in the bathroom mirror packed away till another day.

Static are the morning rooms as I go round them — an unfinished glass of rye, a vase of bronze chrysanthemums, the television doors are open but the drawing-room shows nothing, eternally cool and grave it is like a place in another house. The rooms are linked up by a dark corridor running along the apartment, hung with dubious portraits of unwanted ancestors. At the end is my bedroom, darkest of all and darkened further by the hanging woods of the tapestry facing my bed. I cannot see the colour of my socks in this green gloom.

On the silver tray in the hall (crest of the fighting cock of the Prevosts) are the bills and the invitations. "His Excellency", "the honour", "overdue", and notes of thanks for "a delicious evening". The car is waiting to take me to the office.

Every day and every night this week has been occupied by the Security Council meetings on the Congo. Ever since the Belgians granted independence to the Congo in June that country has been in turmoil. The Belgian officials and technicians cleared out at once, and there are less than a score of Congolese university graduates in the country and no trained officials. The result is chaos. Then Katanga, the province where the copper belt is, seceded from the central government. The Belgians have sent in troops to ensure the evacuation of their remaining nationals and the Russians are accusing them of "imperialist aggression". Now the Secretary-General has been authorized by the Security Council to send a United Nations military force to restore peace there and we are contributing a Canadian signals detachment. My head is woozy with sitting up half the night at these Security Council meetings. My mouth's stale from smoking endless cigarettes, my stomach irritated by nipping out to the bar with my fellow delegates during the translations of speeches. My great friends and allies on these occasions are Freddy Boland, the Irish representative — wise and imperturbable; Nielsen, the Norwegian — a steady friend in all U.N. crises (the Norwegians seem the nearest to the Canadians of any of the Scandinavian delegates, much nearer than the Swedes or the Danes); Jim Plimsoll, the

Australian, and I should say my closest friend at the United Nations — so quick, intelligent, and sensitive. It has been gratifying during the last few days to see how other delegations have rallied round to Canada's defence in the face of persistent attacks on us by the Russians. Yet of course people do inevitably play up to the Russians. That bloody Kuznetsov attacked me personally in the most insolent terms tonight for the support that Canada is giving to Ireland for the presidency of the Assembly. He said this was a Cold War move on our part. I said that he knew perfectly well that our Minister was, as he had so often proved, totally opposed to the Cold War. He replied that in any case Canada had no independence of its own and this was proved by the fact that we were members of NATO. I lost my temper at this, but my temper has got very frail anyway from sitting it out in this vast hot-box of New York, and I also lost my temper with the waiter at the Côte Basque restaurant. Went to a stifling cocktail party at my colleague's, the Indian Representative. God, how tired we are all going to be by the time the coming General Assembly is over! And *what* an Assembly it promises to be, with Khrushchev, Lumumba, Krishna Menon, Nkrumah, and Castro!

September 11, 1960

Things are going from bad to worse in the Congo. The Congolese Premier, Lumumba, has declared that he has lost confidence in the Secretary-General and has demanded the withdrawal of white troops from the U.N. forces. Meanwhile, a mob of Congolese soldiers has attacked and severely beat up fourteen Canadian members in the force at Leopoldville. I have been living much more in the Congo than in New York and it now seems quite possible that I shall be asked to go there. I very much want to do this but I doubt whether it will come off as I think the Russians would object because they disapprove of

Canada, as a member of NATO, having anything to do with the Congo. They are, of course, attacking Hammarskjöld violently. The Scandinavians intend to stick to him through thick and thin.

It is raining. There go the church bells in the rain-soaked air. I have been reading short stories — O. Henry's, Chekov's, and Edgar Allan Poe's — with pleasure, except for Edgar Allan Poe, a writer I have never been able to endure.

September 26, 1960

I have just come in from my morning walk in Central Park and have paid a visit to the macaws and heard the lion giving its waking roar. The Prime Minister* is in New York for the United Nations and has made no effort whatever to contact or consult me. So I sit in my room waiting for a telephone call. I am determined not to approach him. Of course, I should have known what Prime Ministers think of resident ambassadors (when they think of them at all). They simply think that they are "officials" and as such a mixture of flunkey and clerk.

October 3, 1960

When will Butterball (as I now call the maid, Anne) have my breakfast ready? I have to listen to Khrushchev and Menon today at the General Assembly. The Americans have refused the Eisenhower-Khrushchev meeting, and who would have expected them to accept after the wholesale insults fired at them by Khrushchev, whose behaviour is becoming more and more Hitlerian? The spectacle of all these dictators coming here to New York and strutting and orating and bullying reminds one of the Bad Old Days when Hitler and Mussolini were in bloom and busy breaking up the League of Nations. I feel an

*Mr. Diefenbaker.

increasing disgust for what is going on at the United
Nations. The incessant work carries me through time with
the speed of light.

Elizabeth has written to me again encouraging me to
keep my old diaries rather than burn them and to consider
later publication. If I ever do publish them I shall call the
book *Flies Around My Head*. I remember as a small boy
being horrified by the sight of a horse in a field with its
entire face covered with flies and the way it charged up and
down the field trying to shake them off.

The United States Delegation are not at all satisfied
with the Canadian record at this General Assembly. In
fact, I now learn that they have reported that their relations with our Mission here in New York have been so bad
for the last two years and that we (I?) have been so
uncooperative that they have given up approaching us. In
view of my close personal friendship with Cabot Lodge and
the many appreciative things he has said about me, I must
say this surprises me. The truth of the matter is that the
Americans dislike and mistrust the present Canadian government and all its works. Wadsworth, whom I have
known for years and who is now heading the American
Delegation, has never attempted to make the slightest
human contact with me from the first day he arrived here.
The United Nations is full of misunderstandings, worse
this year than ever, and this poisons personal relationships.
People associate their colleagues with the policies of their
respective governments and mistrust the man because they
dislike the policy. This is inevitable but often mistaken.
Half the time the man you think incarnates a hostile
attitude is fighting his own government to get that
attitude changed.

November 27, 1960

Mike Pearson is here today from Ottawa. He and I
had a talk today about the United Nations Secretariat. Last

night he said to someone at dinner, "Charles has done all right. He comes of an old Conservative family and has succeeded in ingratiating himself with the Liberals."

January 1, 1961

Shall we or shall we not go to Haiti for our holiday — that is the question. Matsudiara, the Japanese Ambassador, says, "Don't go near it, it is frightening and sinister," but Loelia Westminster* says, "Yes, go and get me some voodoo charms to braid in my hair the way the Haitian women do." Loelia is here on a visit. How much I like her, her looks and her friendship! I am just going up to drink vodka with her in the blood-red garçonnière which she has been renting.

Matsudiara came into the French Embassy last night, sat down before the fire with a glass of champagne in his hand, looked round the New Year's gathering, and said, "There will be a world war within two years. I have just been telling that to the Japanese press correspondents and I foretold to the month the coming of communism in China. Also," he went on, "there will be communist revolutions in all the Caribbean states." In the wake of these announcements the company paused for station identification. If Matsudiara happened to be right, how would one get the most out of these two years left to us? Madame Schébéko, a White Russian refugee, told me once that if only she had been sure of the date of the coming Soviet revolution she would at once have bought two fur coats and a Rolls-Royce, to get as much satisfaction out of these as possible before all her money was taken away from her.

It is raining! — the darkest, dismallest New York day imaginable, but I continue to love New York in all seasons, and in spite of anything I may say about the United

*Loelia, Duchess of Westminster, now the Hon. Lady Lindsay of Dowhill.

Nations I enjoy being there and would not exchange it for any post in the foreign service.

January 22, 1960

I have been reading Horace Walpole's letters all morning instead of working on our next disarmament resolution. He charms me still as he did when I was a boy of fourteen and read his letters for the first time, when I absurdly wrote that his style was "natural". I think I must have meant "high-spirited". Horace Walpole was troubled by nerve storms but, lucky man, was untroubled so far as we know by the flesh.

Sylvia says that when she is listening to me talking with the Minister on the telephone I come back and say that I have stood up to him and put my views extremely firmly, whereas she had the impression that I agreed with every word he said. A very wifely observation.

Drinks with Charles and Marie Noetbeart. What good friends they are. Marie, unchanged since Ottawa days, as pretty and amusing as ever.

The General Assembly is meeting and yet it is not functioning. Shall we ever extricate ourselves from the morass of the Congo? I still hope so much to go there and have a look at it. The Congo to me has become a country of the mind. I am obsessed by it and more interested in travellers' tales from there than in those from the moon.

Last night I dined at Pat Dean's* with members of the British Delegation. I urged them to use all their influence to get the Belgians, or as many as possible of them, out of the Congo, but I recognized resistance, tenacious, unargumentative. Then the question of barring arms shipments to the Congo came up. Their new Minister came out with, "When one thinks of all the arms being

---

*Sir Patrick Dean, then Permanent Representative of the U.K. to the United Nations; later British Ambassador to the United States.

smuggled all over the world, one wonders why the fuss about arms for the Congo." I thought, "There go we diplomats! If an issue does not suit you, break it up into parts and make it relative. If it comes to that, when one thinks of all the adulteries being committed in the world, what does one adultery matter?"

March 12, 1961

To put myself to sleep I tell myself stories. How flat, trivial, lacking in imagination, and repetitive they are, so that I go to sleep through boredom. By comparison my dreams are works of surrealistic art, brilliant films in the newest continental mode, rich in endless invention, in scenes of hallucinatory brilliance. Even the small "bit parts" in these dreams are rendered with uncanny intensity. As to emotions — fear, love and desolation, danger and narrow escape, lust and nostalgia — the themes are endless and images crowd to express them. If I could tap the sources of dreams, no writer of this age could touch me. There is no doubt I dream like a genius.

At the close of my speech last night Dean Acheson said, "You were superb." "So were you," I replied. "I always am," said Dean.

Walked through the Park to the Plaza Oak Room bar for morning vodka martinis with Sylvia on my arm. She looked lovely, eyes very blue. She has been so patient and sweet during all the storms of the last few months and the strains of the General Assembly. Then we went to the French seventeenth-century exhibition at the Metropolitan, which was badly chosen and arranged. It left an impression of showy, mediocre pictures. Even the Poussins were the poorest I have ever seen; only two Claude Lorrains saved all.

I have been reading Pope's *Rape of the Lock* and now *The Essay on Man* — "In Folly's cup still laughs the bubble Joy".

March 25, 1961 — Washington, D.C.

No, I do not want to come here as Ambassador. Yet if they offered it to me I should probably not refuse it. Why not? Why not tell Norman Robertson that, as a friend, I ask him to save me from it?

As for the brilliant company of the New Frontiersmen and -women, if last night's dinner party is an example I'm afraid it is just a group of clever bureaucrats and their clever or artistic wives meeting after a hard day's work in the office. And must I leave my beloved New York? I feel inclined to make a libation to the Goddess of Liberty at her gates.

Isaiah Berlin, speaking of Adlai Stevenson, told Elizabeth that he hated "a liberal mob". That phrase keeps echoing in my mind irrespective of party labels.

Pope's philosophy is thin and he skates over the depths. It is a day-lit jingle but consider how he slides into poetry and out again. Yet he does not seem to me a religious man like Doctor Johnson. He is a monster of accomplishment rising to genius.

September 18, 1961

A shocking tragedy. Dag Hammarskjöld has been killed in an air accident in the Congo on his way to arrange a cease-fire in the fighting there. Was it an accident? Who will ever know for sure. So many people for so many reasons may have wanted him out of the way. I think his vision of the future of the United Nations will die with him. I also feel his death as a painful personal loss. While he was too detached to be called a friend, I shall so much miss the stimulus of working with him and the pleasure of his companionship.

November 22, 1961 — New York

Lunched today with the Libyans. I sat next to a bearded Oman prince and idiotically asked him how he

liked New York. He said, "It is just like home," and
sniggered slyly.

Coming through the swinging doors of the U.N.
Building I encountered the Romanian Permanent Representative. I have struck up a kind of odd relationship—
almost friendship—with him. He has to return to
Bucharest and says he longs for it. In fact, I am sure he
dreads it. He went on insisting so much about this that it
became embarrassing. Then suddenly that great white
slug seized my arm and said, "I am a human being, you
know." Of course the poor bastard is a human being—
that's his trouble.

The Finnish Ambassador says if you stay long enough
at the United Nations you will find that "all the heels are
wounded." One's skin gets rubbed thin from the close
commerce with one's colleagues in this claustrophobic
place, and as a session of the United Nations goes on,
personal relationships become more and more strained.
Even with my great friend Jim Plimsoll, the Australian, it
was a shock last night, when I voted against the Australian
resolution, seeing his amused, pale, ironic face turn crimson with irritation as he came over to my chair and,
standing over my shoulder, kept repeating, "It's not personal. I know it isn't you, but how *could* you vote the way
you did?"

Before the curtain goes up on the official performance
of the General Assembly and the Councils and Committees
of the United Nations, the scenery has to be put in place,
the parts of the players rehearsed, scripts compared. And
this is done when little groups of actors huddle together in
low-voiced confabulation or drift towards each other casu-
ally—but by arrangement—in the corridors of the Assembly Hall or in the wings of the Security Council. Often
each carries with him a sheet of paper, the text of his
country's forthcoming Resolution, for which he seeks support from other delegations. Or there are points of proce-

dure to be picked over — under which provision would it be best to proceed, or which amendment of the text (often pencilled on the typewritten page) will be most likely to attract support or at least avert defeat by inducing benign abstentions when the Resolution comes to the vote? It is as well to keep these exchanges as inconspicuous as possible, certainly out of earshot of the enemy, for there — on the other side of the lounge — the enemy are gathered in similar preparation for the fray. They are planning the defeat of one's government's cherished project or, more damaging still, an amendment of their own which will, by an extension or rearrangement of language, enlarge the scope of the Resolution and water down its intention so that no credit will redound to your country and there will be no headlines in the press at home to the greater lustre of the government in power.

And now, talking of governments, here comes with soft feet across the carpet towards us an elegant lady, her hair beautifully braided — the multilingual telephonist. "Mr. Ambassador, there is an urgent call for you from the Minister of External Affairs in Ottawa. Would you care to take it now? He is waiting on the line." "Waiting on the line" — that will never do. With hurried apology to my colleagues, with controlled speed — one does not run but moves quietly to the voice of the master — "Hello, Charles. How are things down there? Got everything lined up for our Resolution? Who's supporting — how many co-sponsors?" "What? only nine countries? We'll have to do better than that. What about Australia? No, darn it, we didn't vote for *their* Resolution. India?" "So they want to make it more like an Indian Resolution, do they? Charles, you'll have to get more co-sponsors quickly. I want to make an announcement in the House of Commons tomorrow. Twist a few arms — I know you can do it. Good luck, and let me have the additional names later in the day." It is all very well, but where is one to find these "additional names"? I have already canvassed all those delegations which are in sympathy with our Resolution. I have even incorporated some of their amendments into our text as bait for their support. I wish the Minister was here to twist a few arms himself. No doubt he could do it; he is a practised politician and vote-getter. All day I go from pillar to post seeking out even the most unlikely allies and by late afternoon I am still one short of a total of twelve co-sponsors. But I have reached the end of the line. No one else is interested in the Canadian resolution. I go into the lavatory and, standing at the urinal next to me, buttoning up his trousers, is the Ambassador of Haiti. I barely know the man — our relations with Haiti are minimal. The Duvalier regime is not popular at the United Nations. "Excellency," I say to him in my most polished French, "may I have a word with you?" He looks surprised, almost affronted, at this approach to him in this place. I draw him into the washroom. I do not attempt to explain the merits of our resolution; I simply say, "I am offering Your Excellency a unique opportunity to associate your country with a great initiative in the cause of peace." I venture the suggestion that President Duvalier could not fail to approve. I point out that as the list of co-sponsors appears alphabetically, Haiti would rank high on the printed list, above other important nations. The Ambassador, a small, stout, elephant-coloured man, pauses and stares at me through thick horn-rimmed glasses, and then, "Excellency, I shall have to consult my government." "I fear," I reply, "that the list closes this evening. Would it be possible to have an answer before midnight tonight?" The Ambassador bows and emerges from the washroom. At 11.30 he telephones me — Haiti accepts. I have achieved twelve co-sponsors.

December 9, 1961

I am having difficulties with the Indian Delegation and in particular with the Indian Representative. What prevents him from being what at first sight he seems — a silver-haired, wise Indian civil servant, devoted, highly intelligent, and industrious? What is wrong with him? Why does the oil of malice in him rise so easily to the surface? I should like to know his whole story. Has he been so much snubbed in the past to develop this india-rubbery self-assurance, these ingratiating, pawing gestures? Perhaps that may explain his insistence on his position as an ambassador and his wife's detestable arrogance towards her so-called inferiors. The other night when they dined at this house I put her on my right, on the other side a very intelligent, entertaining member of the Department of External Affairs who is down here on a visit. During the whole of dinner she never spoke one word to him, in fact, turned her back on him. He was not of sufficient rank for her to talk to.

Descartes says that one proof of the existence of God is man's sense of his own imperfection; that this sense of imperfection would not exist unless there were a perfect being. I think of a picture, Piranesi ruins, with some figures of men and women in the foreground. The scale and grandeur of the ruins give the measure of the people, the men and women posed against them illustrate the scale of the walls and pillars. Without God there is no scale of measurement. Man swells into a nervous monster. And yet there are plenty of modest and noble men and women who live without God and plenty of monsters who believe in Him.

January 15, 1962

The die is cast. I am to go as Ambassador to Washington. I suppose I could have flatly said "No", but who would turn down the biggest job in the profession? My hesitation has been partly due to my own blank ignorance of so many of the issues involved between Canada and the

United States, particularly the trade and economic ones.
(When I said this to my mother she replied, "Well, you'll
just have to learn about them, won't you.") I also shrink
from the prospect of returning to normal diplomatic life
with all its tedious formalities and conventionalities. The
United Nations spared one a lot of this. There is little time
for such things in this hothouse of international intrigue,
where one stumbles from crisis to crisis. I prefer this
speeded-up process to a more leisurely pace. However,
perhaps I need not worry about tedium in this new post; on
the contrary, all the storm signals are out for foul weather
between Washington and Ottawa. Relations between the
two governments are bad and show signs of getting worse.
This was brought home to me when I went to Ottawa for
my interview with the Prime Minister on my appointment
and also during my visit to Arnold Heeney, our present
Ambassador in Washington. Not only are there substan-
tive differences of policy involved, but the atmosphere is
poisoned by the mutual aversion of the Prime Minister for
the President and the President for the Prime Minister.
President Kennedy seems to regard Mr. Diefenbaker as a
mischief-making old man who cannot be trusted, whereas
Mr. Diefenbaker sees the President as an arrogant young
man and a political enemy. In such a situation the role of
Canadian Ambassador to Washington promises to be a
tricky one. This does not dismay me, but I ask myself why
I have been selected for it. Arnold Heeney, a warm friend,
has urged that I should be his successor. The Minister,
Howard Green, has adopted me as his candidate for the job
and has been working on the Prime Minister in my favour.
I am grateful for his support; I have always had respect and
affection for him. As for the Prime Minister, I think he
finally made up his mind that I was the safest available bet
for the post, and I wonder whether my Conservative family
connection helped him in my case to overcome his endemic
suspicion of members of the Department of External

Affairs. During our interview I had the impression that he was preoccupied, self-isolated, and, far from enjoying the exercise of power, was overpowered by it.

I hear on all sides that the present government is extremely unpopular in Washington and that the Americans say that every communication they receive from us is a protest or a complaint against them. Also, they are beginning to give us the cold shoulder and their reaction to any Canadian official visitor is a snub. I do not think that this perpetual nattering at the Americans will get us anywhere. I am all for standing up to them on a real question of principle or policy but snapping at their heels all the time is undignified and unproductive. I suppose, however, that they must be getting hardened to this treatment. It is what they get from most of their allies, in intervals of their asking for favours. The British, with their usual realism, ever since the humiliation of Suez, never stop making up to them. At one time we had pretensions to consider ourselves a "bridge" between the United Kingdom and the United States. What a bad joke that looks now! I doubt all the same that the British have much influence on United States policy. The Americans in their present mood do not welcome advice from anyone, least of all from the present Canadian government. I think that one difficulty I shall experience in Washington is finding a basis for communication with the American official world. In the past we have had speedy access to United States government departments on an informal footing which has sometimes been envied by other foreign governments. This has been advantageous to us in some ways but it has its drawbacks. It has meant that our agreement with the general direction of United States policy has been taken for granted, so much so that we hardly seem to be regarded as a "foreign" government at all. When we differ from them on anything important they seem much more surprised and irritated than when dealing with "foreign" countries from whom they can expect trouble. It becomes a sort of family quarrel; always the worst kind. And then, too, the disparity between us has been immensely increased since the War. Now the United States is the greatest military and economic power in the non-communist world, with no British Empire to offset it. The old neighbourly relationship between our two countries was never, of course, based on equality between us, but the inequality was less glaring than it now is.

This enormous access of United States power is reflected inevitably in the men who wield it. A diplomatic colleague who was with me in Washington before the War said the other day, "You will find that the American official has become much 'grander' than he used to be." I have encountered this attitude myself during my visits to Washington but "grand" is not quite the right word for it. The personal friendliness and informality are still there. It is rather that they have developed a complete impermeability to advice, criticism, or comment of any kind, combined with the patient courtesy that one extends to the well-meaning irrelevance. I think that this is an element in the irritation that our Prime Minister feels and that other Canadians may share. No doubt we do not make sufficient allowance for the world-wide responsibilities which the Americans carry on their shoulders. However, any assumption of superiority, conscious or unconscious, has always been peculiarly difficult for Canadians to swallow, prompting the very Canadian question, "Who the hell do they think they are?"

My own problem may be that American friends, knowing of my long association with Mike Pearson, may show a certain sympathy for me in serving under Mr. Diefenbaker. This must be discouraged from the start. I like and admire the Americans, I am devoted to Mike, I shall do anything I can to keep relations on an even keel between Canada and the United States, but if it comes to a showdown of any kind there must be no question as to where my loyalties lie.

January 24, 1962

Farewell party given for us by the San Miniatos.* The Windsors were the feature of the evening. I sat next to her. She has developed a curious, disconcerting tic. When she stops talking, her lips meet and part tremblingly like a nibbling rabbit, or as though she were talking to herself. Indeed, she seems ravaged but unsated, her green eyes brilliant with anticipation of a party at Mrs. Cafritz's† in Washington next week. But then, she is easy, conversable, engagingly full of curiosity, and with a nose tilted for scandal. The Duke, royally red in the face with a white carnation in his buttonhole, expatiated to Sylvia on the impossibility of his having black men to dinner and wondered how we bore this portion of our lot at the United Nations. The room was full of jewels which mattered more than the names and numbers of the players. The Duchess's Schlumberger bracelet of coal-dark sapphires and small diamonds, our hostess's cabochon rubies, my neighbour's enormous black pearl, like a slug crawling over her finger from the foliage of diamonds, and, out-soaring all, the diamond necklace of a Russian lady of endless antecedents, whose still-lovely face is permanently framed in an envelope of gauze. "Does she take it off," they asked her husband, "when she goes to bed?" "No, never," he replied, "but it isn't that that I mind. It is that her diamonds scratch." Café society is not a cinch. These people bought or charmed or clawed their way into this enclosure. There is less room for nonentities here than in ordinary society. The room is full of adventurers and adventuresses, from born ladies who got sick of being

*The Duke and Duchess of San Miniatos. The Duchess is Canadian by birth.

†Well-known Washington hostess of the period.

ladies to slightly shop-worn countesses from Brooklyn or the Bronx, and one white-skinned young beauty with a pile of red hair and sardonic eyes. This is a slippery arena and I was glad to see my dear friend, our hostess, dauntless Gladys, steering her way with a certain rough, tough, shy, bold authority.

April 2, 1962

As my departure from New York becomes imminent, I have been reflecting on the United Nations and its claim to be a world community — and on the tragic fate of Dag Hammarskjöld. The world community was to be incarnated in the United Nations, but the incarnation has never really taken place. Its prophet — and, since his death in the Congo, its martyr — was Dag Hammarskjöld. Its religious ceremony, so it seems to me, is the concert of classical music (chosen by Dag) which is the prelude to the meeting of the General Assembly. There are the delegates from more than half the world gathered together — for once in silence — with reverent expressions on their faces, listening to the strains of Beethoven and Bach, their souls presumably lifted above mundane differences into an ethereal world of music in which their common humanity is made manifest. The concert lasts about an hour — the unity of mood among the listeners lasts no longer. There is also the chapel or room of meditation — undenominational, of course — to which it must have been hoped that delegates would repair to cool their tempers exacerbated in the heat of debate and to contemplate the latter end of things. I have looked in there once or twice myself. On those occasions it was empty, except for a member of the U.N. security guard pacing up and down at the entrance, to guard it against defilement.

There used to be a common saying — I forget who originated it — that "the United Nations is no better than its members". That indeed was a truism abundantly proved, but the very fact that it had to be stated shows that there is a widespread expectation — or at least hope — that the whole will turn out to be more than its parts. There is support for the cause of the United Nations (nowhere more than in Canada), and this cause is felt to be something superior to the sum total of the different nations represented there. It is to be an emanation of the good intentions, the better selves, of these nations, working together for peace and the dignity of man. A spirit brooding upon the waters of a troubled world. Of course, many of those who devote themselves to the cause are hard-headed, able men and women, not easily deluded by optimism but sustained by a purpose. There is, however, an element of mysticism and also of muddle in the minds of many of its supporters. They expect miracles and are disillusioned. For this, Hammarskjöld himself — the symbol of the United Nations — bore some of the responsibility. He himself was a mystic but he was far from muddled. Like Mahatma Gandhi, who in some ways he resembled, he combined a fervent faith in the unseen with a very keen eye for the scene before him. He knew — none better — the task he had set himself and he approached it with spiritual humility and intellectual arrogance. The task was to speed the evolution of the United Nations from a meeting-place of nations into an effective instrument in international politics — to make of it what some mistakenly believe it already is, a cohesive force. He knew that the odds were against him, but he had been a mountaineer. Over the fireplace in his own room was suspended a mountaineer's pick — it was not there for nothing. He would set out to scale the mountain and if he failed to reach the top the fall would be precipitous. This was the risk that added zest to the enterprise. Meanwhile, like any experienced climber, he would assess the chances, study the terrain, and hire the most trustworthy guides — his own secretariat. The mountain that he set himself to conquer was that of exclusive, aggressive nationalism, deeply rooted in history and engendering conflict. For all his skills, it proved too much for him. His failure can be attributed too simply to Soviet resistance. This was the precipitant, but it was also a convenient screen for the reluctance of others, especially the Western Great Powers, to accord him the support he would have needed. How then did he go wrong? It was partly a failure of patience, partly an overplaying of his hand. These were the political errors. Beyond them was a deeper failure — the failure of the doctrine he sought to embody — the doctrine of supernational solidarity. It was too insubstantial — too fleshless; it might take hold of men's minds but could not appeal to their passions. The air at the top of the mountain was too thin for common humans.

April 27, 1962

It is half an hour before train time, the suitcases are packed. There is no necessity for me to lug them all into the hall — that is precisely what we gave five dollars to the doorman to do — but I know I shall be pressured into doing it myself. Before breakfast this morning I went for a farewell walk in the Park and, standing on the bridge, quickly and sadly said goodbye to my beloved New York. It has served me well and would have done even better for me if I had had more initiative to plunder its gifts. I shall never in any foreseeable or unforeseeable future live in this place again. It is painful to leave, but this must be concealed from Washingtonians, as they no more appreciate hearing good things of New York than New Yorkers do of Washington.

Index